TERMS OF TRADE

The Language of International Trade Policy, Law, and Diplomacy

Edited by
Thomas F. O'Herron

International Advisory Services Group, Ltd.
Consumers For World Trade - Education Fund

Publisher's Cataloging-in-Publication
(Provided by Quality Books, Inc.)

Terms of trade : the language of international trade policy, law, and diplomacy / edited by Thomas F. O'Herron. -- 2nd ed.
p. cm.
LCCN: 97-74868
ISBN: 0-9624861-0-8

1. International economic relations--Dictionaries. 2. International trade--Dictionaries. I. O'Herron, Thomas F.

HF1373.T73 1999 337.03
QBI99-248

Published by IAS Publishing, 1707 L St., NW, Suite 725, Washington D.C. 20036

Cover Design by Carol Nansel, Imtek Office Solutions
Printed in the U.S.A. by Cavanaugh Press, Inc.

In Memory of Gardner Patterson

We dedicate this edition to the memory of Gardner Patterson (1916-1998), in recognition of his invaluable contributions to the promotion of international trade.

After service in the U.S. Navy in World War II, Mr. Patterson earned a Ph.D. from Harvard University, then joined the faculty of Princeton University, where he served from 1949 to 1973. During that period, Mr. Patterson also accepted special assignments in support of the economic development of Greece, Turkey, and Tunisia. In 1973, he was named Deputy Director of the General Agreement on Tariffs and Trade, a position he held until 1981.

Preface

Over the past fifty years, the world has moved away from nationalistic isolationism and protectionism and toward a cooperative, more integrated global trading environment, by eliminating many barriers to trade and establishing international rules of fair play among trading nations. Trade has become an engine for economic growth and a key component of economic development.

Growth of trade has exceeded that of output by a substantial amount over the past 50 years. In 1950, 7 percent of global GDP moved in international trade; today, over 23 percent does. Since the first General Agreement on Tariffs and Trade (GATT) negotiations in 1947, average tariffs among industrialized countries have dropped from high double-digit levels to less than 4 percent. In 1947, 23 countries took part in the GATT; today, there are 133 Members in the GATT's successor, the World Trade Organization (WTO), with 30 additional nations awaiting consideration.

Developing countries are responsible for one-quarter of world trade; ten years ago they accounted for less than one-fifth. Their share of trade in manufactured goods alone has doubled to 20 percent from 10 percent. Over 90 preferential regional agreements are in existence today, more than three-quarters of which entered into force within the last four years. As of mid-1998, about 120 disputes had been presented to the WTO for resolution in the four years since its inception, compared to just over 300 over the entire lifetime of the GATT (1948-1994).

These considerations serve to underscore the expanding central position world trade holds in international affairs, as well as in our everyday lives. Given these facts, it becomes increasingly necessary for people from all walks of life to be familiar with the specialized language used in the conduct of trade.

This glossary contains what we hope are clear, concise, and readable definitions of the most important terms used in international trade, United States trade legislation, and international business.

Glossary entries include cross references, historical background, and examples in cases where a need for clarity or completeness seemed to call for them. In addition, a number of unconventional terms have been included in an effort to pierce the veil of insider jargon.

This edition of Terms of Trade has more than doubled the size of the first edition, with more than 350 new terms, in an effort to incorporate all the pertinent terminology relating to the dramatic events of the last 8 years. Although we have dropped some terms no longer in use and with no enduring significance, we retained a number of historical terms which we deemed necessary to a proper understanding of world trade today. This text has been updated to encompass terms relating to the European Union, the WTO, NAFTA, economies in transition, and more, in addition to an extensive listing of acronyms and abbreviations. The appendices have been expanded and revised to include a chronological ordering of GATT Rounds; an outline of the WTO Agreement and list of current WTO Members; a brief description of the European Union (EU), its institutions, members, and milestones marking its growth and integration; a complete listing of the 13 Incoterms, the standardized terms and conditions of sale codified by the International Chamber of Commerce (ICC); timetables for U.S. antidumping and countervailing duty investigation proceedings; and an extensive listing of websites maintained by government agencies, international organizations, and trade associations.

We are confident that this edition will be a valuable tool for people in government and commerce; teachers and students of international trade; business people who import or export; and journalists and others who are called upon to explain, use or merely understand the vital but often obscure language of international trade policy, law, and diplomacy.

Charles Blum deserves credit for conceiving this project, recruiting a talented team of researchers, and guiding them along a steep learning curve. His enthusiasm and dedication were crucial to the completion of the project. Melissa Walters worked with unflagging diligence and resourcefulness for months, checking facts, uncovering reliable sources of information, drafting scores of items, arranging the entire manuscript, and proofreading each successive draft. John Buda, Amy Houpt and Pinar Taskin also researched, wrote, revised and proofread substantial portions of the manuscript. Their assistance hastened the completion of the project and enhanced its quality.

When specialized knowledge was needed, the team was able to turn to a number of experts who generously gave of their time and expertise: Ned Marshak, Mike Hathaway, Sibylle Frucht, Mark Paulson, and Bonnie Richardson. Special thanks are also due to Mike Robertson and Kate Lannan, who provided a wealth of information on Canadian trade law and regulations.

The breadth and depth of the revisions were guided by the invaluable recommendations of the members of the Advisory Committee, each an outstanding practitioner in the field, that was established in support of this project, in conjunction with the Consumers for World Trade Educational Foundation. Advisory Committee members Joseph Greenwald, Charles Heeter, Gary Hufbauer, Julius Katz, Lewis Leibowitz, Eliza Patterson, Gardner Patterson and Ritchie Thomas each reviewed the first edition and recommended items for inclusion, deletion and revision. We are grateful for their assistance in launching this project.

Note to the Reader:

In WTO usage, countries which belong to the organization are referred to as Members (upper case M). We have used the less formal "members" (lower case m) in this handbook.

Advisory Committee

International Advisory Services Group and Consumers for World Trade - Education Fund would like to thank the members of their Advisory Committee for their help.

Joseph Greenwald
Michael Hathaway
Charles Heeter
Gary Hufbauer
Julius Katz
Lewis Leibowitz
Eliza Patterson
Gardner Patterson
Ritchard Thomas

INTRODUCTION
by
CONSUMERS FOR WORLD TRADE

Terms of Trade is being published at a propitious time. One of the few matters in the national trade debate on which there is a consensus is that there is an alarming lack of knowledge and a great deal of misunderstanding about trade among both novices and professionals. As we move deeper into a global economy, it is becoming increasingly necessary to enhance trade awareness among the general public as well as among the formulators and implementers of trade policy.

Certainly, there is today a deluge of in-depth trade information available from such sources as government and private sector reports, press articles and television programs, not to mention cyberspace. However, seldom is all this material found in a compact format and in language understandable to everyone. We hope that Terms of Trade, its glossary and appendices, will provide such a tool and facilitate the work of both the learner and the instructor.

In response to this need for better understanding of the trade process, Consumers for World Trade (CWT), a national, non-profit organization established in 1978, created the Consumers for World Trade Educational Fund (CWT-EF) in 1981. CWT-EF is dedicated solely to educating the American public about international trade – how it works and why it is important - the value of global commerce to the national economy as well as to the daily life of every individual.

CWT-EF's current initiative focuses on the high school student, a voracious consumer and future decision-maker. The High School Trade Education Project has four goals:

- To foster an interest in international trade among young consumers;
- To develop student awareness of how the international trading

system affects young people;
- To better prepare students for their future in a global economy by exposing them to international trade at an early age; and
- To encourage teachers to incorporate international trade issues into their regular curricula.

To achieve these goals, CWT-EF is distributing to schools around the country a textbook written especially for young students: "Trade is Everybody's Business." In the near future, the Fund will develop additional teaching tools such as classroom simulation and video materials.

But students are not the only ones that are in need of help in deciphering the complexities of international trade. Many of us, in both the public and private sectors, though we may have been involved in the trade field for many years, cannot recall the date and details of a particular trade agreement, what Article XIV of the GATT is all about, or the difference between IPAC and ISAC. We hope, therefore, that Terms of Trade will both find its way to educational institutions around the country and become as well a fixture on the desks of trade professionals as a dependable and easy-to-use reference tool.

The parent organization of CWT-EF, Consumers for World Trade, is dedicated to representing the consumer interest in international trade. It does so through advocacy of trade expansion and trade liberalization. Its mission is to promote healthy economic growth, provide consumer choice in the marketplace, and counteract inflationary price increases brought about by the erection of tariff and non-tariff barriers.

CWT testifies before the legislative and executive branches, reminding the formulators of trade policy of the benefits of an open trading system. It participates on trade advisory bodies and in international conferences. In order to keep the public informed, CWT publishes newsletters, consumer alerts and other informative materials; sends out press releases; submits letters to periodicals for publication; and conducts regular forums on current trade issues.

In addition, CWT reaches out to university students through its affiliated

Students for World Trade (SWT) clubs on college campuses. SWT encourages its members to discuss trade topics and, through a variety of programs, provides students with an opportunity to be part of the public's voice when trade policies are being formulated.

You may learn more about the organization, its activities, its positions on trade issues and its membership options by visiting the CWT web site at http://www.cwt.org, or by contacting us by phone at (202) 785-4835 or e-mail at cwt@cwt.org.

Table of Contents

List of Abbreviations ix-xvii

Terms A - Z 1-173

Appendices

I. WTO Agreement 174

II. WTO Members 179

III. GATT Rounds 185

IV. Major U.S. Trade Policy Legislation 188

V. Antidumping and Countervailing Duty Investigation Timetables 196

VI. European Union 198

VII. Incoterms 203

VIII. Useful Websites 207

Abbreviations

ABI	Automated Broker Interface
ACP	African, Caribbean, and Pacific Countries
ACS	Association of Caribbean States
ACTPN	Advisory Committee on Trade Policy and Negotiations (U.S.)
ACV	Agreement on Customs Valuation
Ad Ref	Ad Referendum
AD	Anti-dumping
ADB	Asian Development Bank
AfDB	African Development Bank
AGP	Agreement on Government Procurement
AID	Agency for International Development (U.S.)
ALADI	Latin American Integration Association
AMS	Aggregate Measure of Support
ANSI	American National Standards Institute
ANZCERTA	Australia-New Zealand Closer Economic Relations Trade Agreement
APAC	Agriculture Policy Advisory Committee
APEC	Asian-Pacific Economic Cooperation
APO	Administrative Protective Order
APTA	Automotive Products Trade Agreement
ASEAN	Association of South East Asian Nations
ATC	Agreement on Textiles and Clothing
ATCA	Agreement on Trade in Civil Aircraft
ATPA	Andean Trade Preference Act

AVE	Ad Valorem Equivalent
BAA	Buy America Act
BEMs	Big Emerging Markets
BIA	Built-In Agenda
BIAC	Business and Industry Advisory Committee
BIT	Bilateral Investment Treaty
BOP	Balance of Payments
BOT	Balance of Trade
BPI	Business Proprietary Information
BTN	Brussels Tariff Nomenclature
BTS	Basic Telecommunications Service
BXA	Bureau of Export Administration
C & F	Cost and Freight
CACEU	Central African Customs and Economic Union
CACM	Central American Common Market
CAD	Cash Against Documents
CAP	Common Agricultural Policy of the European Union
CAR	Commercial Activity Report
CARICOM	Caribbean Economic Community
CBD	Commerce Business Daily
CBERA	Caribbean Basin Economic Recovery Act
CBI	Caribbean Basin Initiative
CCC	Commodity Credit Corporation
CCC	Customs Cooperation Council
CCCN	Customs Cooperation Council Nomenclature
CCL	Commerce Control List
CEA	Chinese Economic Area
CEA	Council of Economic Advisors (U.S.)
CEFTA	Central European Free Trade Agreement
CER	Closer Economic Relations

CFIUS	Committee on Foreign Investment in the United States
CIF	Cost, Insurance, and Freight
CIITC	Commission on International Investment and Transnational Corporations
CIS	Commonwealth of Independent States
CIT	Court of International Trade
CITA	Committee for Implementation of Textile Agreements
CoCom	Coordinating Committee on Multilateral Export Controls
COMECON	Council for Mutual Economic Assistance
COREPER	Committee of Permanent Representatives of the European Union
CPs	Contracting Parties
CRA	Committee on Regional Arrangements
CSE	Consumer Subsidy Equivalent
CSUSTL	Committee to Strengthen U.S. Trade Laws
CTA	Committee on Trade in Agriculture
CTD	Committee on Trade and Development
CTE	Common Trade Environment
CTG	Council for Trade in Goods
CTIS	Center For Trade and Investment Services
CVD	Countervailing Duty
CWO	Cash With Order
CXT	Common External Tariff
DEIP	Dairy Export Incentive Program
DISC	Domestic International Sales Corporation
DOC	Department of Commerce (U.S.)
DSB	Dispute Settlement Body
DSU	Dispute Settlement Understanding
EAI	Enterprises for the Americas Initiative
EARB	Export Administration Review Board
EBB	Economic Bulletin Board

EBRD	European Bank for Reconstruction and Development
EC	European Communities
ECSC	European Coal and Steel Community
ECU	European Currency Unit
EEC	European Economic Community
EEZ	Exclusive Economic Zone
EFTA	European Free Trade Association
EMS	European Monetary System
EMU	European [and or Economic] Monetary Union
EPC	Economic Policy Council
ER	Export Restraint
ERM	Exchange Rate Mechanism
EU	European Union
EURATOM	European Atomic Energy Community
EXIMBANK	Export-Import Bank
FDI	Foreign Direct Investment
FIRA	Foreign Investment Review Act [or Agency]
FOB	Free on Board
FOGS	Functioning of the GATT System
FSC	Foreign Sales Corporation
FTA	Free Trade Agreement
FTA	Free Trade Area
FTAA	Free Trade Agreement of the Americas
GAL	Guaranteed Access Level
GATS	General Agreement on Trade in Services
GATT	General Agreement on Tariffs and Trade
GCC	Gulf Cooperation Council
GDP	Gross Domestic Product
GEF	Global Environmental Facility
GIIC	Global Information Infrastructure Commission
GMO	Genetically Modified Organism

GNP	Gross National Product
GSP	Generalized System of Preferences
HS	Harmonized System
IAP	Individual Action Plan
IBRD	International Bank for Reconstruction and Development (the World Bank)
ICC	International Chamber of Commerce
ICJ	International Court of Justice
IDA	International Development Agency
IDB	Inter-American Development Bank
IEEPA	International Emergency Economic Powers Act
IFAC	Industry Function Advisory Committee
IFC	International Finance Corporation
IFI	International Financial Institutions
IGC	Intergovernmental Conference
IIC	Inter-American Investment Corporation
ILO	International Labor Organization
ILP	Import Licensing Programs
ILSA	Iran-Libya Sanctions Act
IMF	International Monetary Fund
INR	Initial Negotiating Right
INRA	International Natural Rubber Agreement
IPAC	Industry Policy Advisory Committee
IPRs	Intellectual Property Rights
ISAC	Industry Sector Advisory Committee
ISO	International Standards Organization
IT	Information Technology
ITA	Information Technology Agreement
ITA	International Trade Administration
ITC	International Trade Commission
ITO	International Trade Organization
ITTA	International Tropical Timber Agreement

ITU	International Telecommunications Union
JCIT	Joint Committee for Investment and Trade
JETRO	Japan External Trade Organization
KITA	Korean International Trade Association
KOTRA	Korea Trade Promotion Corporation
L/C	Letter of Credit
LAFTA	Latin American Free Trade Association
LAIA	Latin American Integration Association
LDCs	Less Developed Countries
LIBOR	London Interbank Offered Rate
LIFFE	London International Financial Futures and Options Exchange
LSAC	Labor Sector Advisory Committee
LTA	Long Term Agreement on International Trade in Cotton Textiles
LTFV	Less Than Fair Value
LTOM	London Traded Options Market
MAI	Multilateral Agreement on Investment
MEA	Multilateral Environmental Agreement
MFA	Multi-Fibre Arrangement
MFN	Most Favored Nation
MIF	Multilateral Investment Fund
MIGA	Multilateral Investment Guarantee Agency
MITI	Ministry of International Trade and Industry (Japan)
MOP	Margin of Preference
MOSS	Market-Oriented, Sector-Specific (Talks)
MOU	Memorandum of Understanding
MPP	Market Promotion Program
MRA	Mutual Recognition Agreement
MSA	Multilateral Steel Agreement
MSSA	Multilateral Specialty Steel Agreement
MTN	Multilateral Trade Negotiations

NAFTA	North American Free Trade Agreement
NAICS	North American Industry Classification System
NEC	National Economic Council
NGO	Non-Governmental Organization
NICs	Newly Industrializing Countries
NIEs	Newly Industrializing Economies
NIS	Newly Independent States (of the former Soviet Union)
NME	Non-Market Economy
NTB	Non-Tariff Barrier
NTM	Non-Tariff Measure
NTR	Normal Trade Relations
OAS	Organization of American States
OAU	Organization of African Unity
ODTC	Office of Defense Trade Controls
OECD	Organization for Economic Cooperation and Development
OECS	Organization of Eastern Caribbean States
OFAC	Office of Foreign Assets Controls
OMAs	Orderly Marketing Arrangements
OPEC	Organization of Petroleum Exporting Countries
OPIC	Overseas Private Investment Corporation
OTEXA	Office of Textiles, Apparel and Consumer Goods
PFC	Priority Foreign Country
PFP	Policy Framework Paper
PPA	Protocol of Provisional Application
PPMs	Processing and Production Methods
PPP	Purchasing Power Parity
PSE	Producer Subsidy Equivalent
PSI	Preshipment Inspection

PWL	Priority Watch List
QR	Quantitative Restriction or Restraint
RBP	Restrictive Business Practice
S&D	Special and Differential (Treatment of Developing Countries)
SAARC	South Asian Association for Regional Cooperation
SADC	Southern Africa Development Community
SCM	Agreement on Subsidies and Countervailing Measures
SDR	Special Drawing Right
SICS	Standard Industrial Classification System
SIS	Security of Information Systems
STE	State Trading Enterprise
TABD	Transatlantic Business Dialogue
TBR	Trade Barriers Regulation
TDA	Trade Development Agency
TEA	Trade Expansion Act of 1962
TEP	Transatlantic Economic Partnership
TEPAC	Trade and Environmental Policy Advisory Committee
TIB	Temporary Importation Under Bond
TMB	Textile Monitoring Board
TNC	Trade Negotiating Committee
TPC	Trade Policy Committee
TPL	Tariff Preference Level
TPM	Trigger Price Mechanism
TPRG	Trade Policy Review Group
TPRM	Trade Policy Review Mechanism
TPSC	Trade Policy Staff Committee
TRIMs	Trade-Related Investment Measures
TRIPs	Trade-Related Aspects of Intellectual Property Protection

TSB	Textile Surveillance Board
TSUS	Tariff Schedules of the United States
TVA	Tax on Value Added
TWN	Third World Network
UMA	Arab Maghreb Union
UNCITRAL	United Nations Commission on International Trade Law
UNCTAD	United Nations Conference on Trade and Development
UNCTC	United Nations Centre on Transnational Corporations
UNEP	United Nations Environmental Programme
UNIDO	United Nations Industrial Development Organization
USITC	United States International Trade Commission
USML	United States Munitions List
USTR	United States Trade Representative
VAT	Value Added Tax
VER	Voluntary Export Restraint
VRA	Voluntary Restraint Agreement
WCO	World Customs Organization
WHO	World Health Organization
WIPO	World Intellectual Property Organization
WTO	World Trade Organization

A

ABSOLUTE ADVANTAGE - The trade theory concept associated with Adam Smith which says that a country will export those goods it can produce at a lower cost (in terms of labor and other inputs) than other countries. *See Comparative Advantage*

ACCESSION - In the context of the World Trade Organization (WTO), the process by which a state or separate customs territory may become a Member. In WTO usage, a country which belongs to the organization is commonly referred to as a Member (upper case M). The new Member's commitments are to apply equally to all WTO members under normal non-discrimination rules, even though they are negotiated bilaterally with principal trading partners. Accession to the WTO requires that the new Member be bound by the WTO Agreement and all of the multilateral agreements *(see Appendix I)*. Final acceptance is contingent upon a two-thirds majority of WTO members voting in favor. In some cases, the country's own parliament or legislature has to ratify the agreement before membership is complete. In the European Union, the process by which a country becomes a member. *See Appendix VI*

ACCOUNTING RATE - With reference to telephone service, the price a U.S. carrier negotiates with a foreign carrier for handling one minute of international telephone service.

ACQUIS COMMUNAUTAIRE -The community patrimony, i.e., the body of treaties, supplementary instruments, and secondary legislation that establishes the rights and obligations of European Union Member States.

ACTIONABLE SUBSIDY - A subsidy which benefits exports, and which may be subject to countervailing measures under the WTO Agreement on Subsidies and Countervailing Measures *(see entry)* because of its adverse effects on the interests of other Members. Adverse effects are defined as injury to the domestic industry of another Member, nullification or impairment of benefits accruing to other Members under GATT 94, or serious prejudice to the interests of another Member. Any of these effects is grounds for dispute settlement. On the basis of an adverse ruling, a Member found to be granting an actionable subsidy may remove its adverse effects or offer compensation in the form of trade concessions on other goods. Failing that, the affected Member may be authorized to take countermeasures commensurate with the harm which the subsidy has caused. *See Countervailable Subsidy, Non-actionable Subsidy, Prohibited Subsidy*

ADJUSTMENT ASSISTANCE - Financial and technical assistance to firms, workers, and communities designed to help them adjust to rising import competition. Adjustment assistance can help firms become more efficient and can facilitate shifts of resources from less productive to more productive industries. For example, under U.S. law, workers adversely affected by increased import competition may receive special unemployment compensation, retraining to develop new skills, and job search and relocation assistance; affected firms may receive technical assistance and loan guarantees to finance their modernization or shift to other product lines; and communities threatened by increasing imports may receive loans and other assistance to attract new industry or to enable existing plants to move into more competitive fields.

ADMINISTERING AUTHORITY - In the context of U.S. antidumping and countervailing duty proceedings, the Department of Commerce.

ADMINISTRATIVE GUIDANCE - The system of informal but influential suggestions used by the Japanese Government as an instrument of industrial policy.

ADMINISTRATIVE PROTECTIVE ORDER (APO) - In the context of antidumping and countervailing duty proceedings of the U.S. Department of Commerce and U.S. International Trade Commission, a procedure by which the confidentiality of business proprietary information is ensured. Information subject to an APO may be disclosed only to authorized persons, primarily attorneys.

ADMINISTRATIVE REVIEW - In the context of administrative trade proceedings of the U.S. Department of Commerce, an annual update of any antidumping or countervailing duty order. The Commerce Department's International Trade Administration is required to conduct such a review upon the request of any interested party.

AD REFERENDUM (Ad Ref) - Subject to the agreement of superior authority. "Ad Ref" is used during the process of negotiating agreements or concessions. If something is agreed "Ad Referendum" by negotiators on the scene, it is understood that the matter requires the final approval of a higher governmental authority.

AD VALOREM EQUIVALENT (AVE) - A "specific" duty which is expressed as a percentage of the value of an import. Thus, a duty of $l per shirt on shirts valued at $10 each has an AVE of 10%. Where tariffs are reduced on a percentage basis, AVEs must be calculated to permit proportional cuts in specific duties. *See Specific Tariff*

AD VALOREM TARIFF - A tariff assessed as a percentage of the value of the goods cleared through customs. For example, 10% ad valorem means the tariff is 10% of the value of the goods.

ADVISORY COMMITTEE ON TRADE POLICY AND NEGOTIATIONS (ACTPN) - An advisory committee to the U.S. Government, consisting of no more than 45 members, broadly representative of U.S. economic interests, appointed by the President for two year terms, upon nomination of the United States Trade Representative. The ACTPN may establish task forces on specific trade policy issues on which it reports with recommendations. Prior to the conclusion of any negotiation, the committee is required to produce a written report with conclusions, which is forwarded to the Congress at the time the agreement is submitted for approval.

AFRICAN, CARIBBEAN AND PACIFIC COUNTRIES (ACP) - The 71 countries, mostly former colonies of member states of the European Union (EU), which receive financial and technical assistance, as well as certain trade benefits, from the EU under the Lomé Convention *(see entry).*

AFRICAN DEVELOPMENT BANK (AfDB) - A multilateral institution established to assist in the economic and social development of African nations, and to promote economic cooperation among them. In addition to African countries, the AfDB membership includes Japan, the United States, and other Western donor countries.

AFRICAN ECONOMIC COMMUNITY (AEC) - A branch of the Organization of African Unity (see entry) created in June 1991 to promote the economic, social, and cultural development and integration of African economies in an effort to foster greater self-sufficiency and self reliance among participating nations. The AEC has 53 members and may be joined by any member of the OAU.

AGGREGATE MEASURE OF SUPPORT (AMS) - A monetary measure of the support provided to agricultural production by means of governmental outlays to producers, or by means of government revenue forgone. This measure is sometimes referred to by its French name, *le montant de soutien.*

AGREEMENT ON AGRICULTURE - One of the international accords adopted in 1994 as part of the Final Act Embodying the Results of the Uruguay Round of Multilateral Trade Negotiations. The agreement requires reductions in domestic support for agricultural production and export subsidies on agricultural products, the conversion of non-tariff measures to tariffs, and across-the-board reductions of tariffs.

AGREEMENT ON ANTI-DUMPING - Formally, the Agreement on Implementation of Article VI of the General Agreement on Tariffs and Trade 1994. An international trade accord, adopted in 1994 as part of the Final Act Embodying the Results of the Uruguay Round of Multilateral Trade Negotiations, which replaces the Anti-dumping Code negotiated in the GATT's Tokyo Round. The agreement establishes both substantive and procedural standards for national antidumping proceedings.

AGREEMENT ON CUSTOMS VALUATION - Formally, the Agreement on Implementation of Article VII of the General Agreement on Tariffs and Trade 1994. Negotiated in the Uruguay Round of Multilateral Trade Negotiations, this agreement replaces the Customs Valuation Code negotiated in the GATT's Tokyo Round. The agreement provides detailed rules for the determination of value for customs purposes, designed to provide a fair, uniform, and neutral system of valuation based on transaction value.

AGREEMENT ON GOVERNMENT PROCUREMENT- An international trade agreement, first negotiated during the Tokyo Round and effective as of January 1, 1981, by which signatories agree to open government purchasing to international competition on a reciprocal basis. It is designed to make laws, regulations, procedures, and practices regarding government procurement more transparent; and to define and restrict the permissible ways in which government purchases may be used to protect domestic products or suppliers, or discriminate against foreign products or suppliers. As of mid-1998, parties to the agreement include Aruba (Netherlands), Austria, Belgium, Canada, Denmark, European Union, Finland, France, Germany, Greece, Hong Kong (China), Ireland, Israel, Italy, Japan, Korea, Liechtenstein, Luxembourg, Netherlands,Norway, Portugal, Singapore, Spain, Sweden, Switzerland, United Kingdom, and United States. *See Plurilateral Agreements*

AGREEMENT ON IMPLEMENTATION OF ARTICLE VI - *See Agreement on Anti-dumping*

AGREEMENT ON IMPORT LICENSING PROCEDURES - *See Import Licensing Code*

AGREEMENT ON INTERPRETATION AND APPLICATION OF ARTICLES VI, XVI, AND XXIII - *See Agreement on Subsidies and Countervailing Measures*

AGREEMENT ON PRESHIPMENT INSPECTION (PSI) - A WTO agreement governing the use, primarily by developing countries, of specialized private companies to carry out inspections of goods destined for export. PSIs verify prices, quantities, and the quality of shipments before they leave the exporting nation. The agreement recognizes that GATT principles and obligations apply to the activities of preshipment inspection agencies. The obligations placed on PSI-user governments include non-discrimination, transparency, protection of confidential business information, avoidance of unreasonable delays, specific guidelines for conducting price verification, and the avoidance of conflicts of interest by PSI agencies.

AGREEMENT ON SUBSIDIES AND COUNTERVAILING MEASURES (SCM) - A WTO agreement which defines the use of subsidies and regulates the actions that countries can take to counter the effects of subsidies. This agreement builds on and substantially revises the Tokyo Round Subsidies Code (formally known as the "Agreement on Interpretation and Application of Articles VI, XVI and XXIII"). *See Actionable Subsidy, Non-Actionable Subsidy, Prohibited Subsidy*

AGREEMENT ON TECHNICAL BARRIERS TO TRADE - One of the international trade agreements negotiated in the Uruguay Round of Multilateral Trade Negotiations and approved in 1994. This agreement expands and improves on the Standards Code negotiated in the Tokyo Round. The Agreement is designed to eliminate trade barriers in the form of national product standards and testing practices, while permitting members to protect the health, safety, environmental and consumer interests of their citizens.

AGREEMENT ON TEXTILES AND CLOTHING (ATC) - A WTO agreement providing for the phased liberalization and elimination of quotas on textiles and apparel imported from WTO Member Countries. This agreement was approved by the United States as part of the Uruguay Round Agreements Act and went into effect on January 1, 1995. Article 2 of the Agreement states that the phase-out of the Multi-Fibre Arrangement (MFA) *(see entry)* quotas, and the acceleration of quota growth rates, are to be implemented in three stages over ten years.

AGREEMENT ON THE APPLICATION OF SANITARY AND PHYTOSANITARY MEASURES - A WTO agreement concerning food, animal, and plant health regulations. The Agreement recognizes that governments have the right to take sanitary and phytosanitary measures, including trade restrictions, to protect human, animal, or plant life if the measures are based upon sufficient scientific evidence. The Agreement seeks to limit such measures to those actually needed for that purpose. ("Phytosanitary" refers to plant health.)

AGREEMENT ON TRADE IN CIVIL AIRCRAFT (ATC) - An international aviation accord which eliminates import duties on non-military aircraft, engines, parts, components, and sub-assemblies, as well as on flight simulators, their parts and components. The agreement also establishes disciplines on government support for sale of civil aircraft, as well as on government financial support for the civil aircraft sector. The agreement entered into force on January 1, 1980. As of mid 1998, signatories to the agreement include Austria, Belgium, Bulgaria, Canada, Denmark, Egypt, European Union, Finland, France, Germany, Greece, Ireland, Italy, Japan, Luxembourg, Netherlands, Norway, Portugal, Romania, Spain, Sweden, Switzerland, Taiwan, United Kingdom, and United States.

AGRICULTURE POLICY ADVISORY COMMITTEE (APAC) - A body of agriculture experts which, pursuant to the mandate of the U.S. Trade and Tariff Act of 1984, advises the U.S. Trade Representative and the U.S. Department of Agriculture on the agricultural aspects of multilateral trade negotiations.

AIRCRAFT AGREEMENT - Formally known as the "Agreement on Trade in Civil Aircraft" (ATCA) *(see entry).*

AMERICAN GOODS RETURNED - A term of art for products exported to the U.S. that are later returned without having been "advanced in value or improved in condition" while abroad. Such goods may be returned to the U.S. free of duty under HTS subheading 9801.00.10. For example, a shipment of goods might be exported for sorting or repackaging, and then returned to the U.S. without payment of duty. Other special duty exemptions are provided for under HTS subheading 9802 for certain goods that have been repaired, altered, processed, or assembled abroad. *See Maquiladora System*

AMERICAN NATIONAL STANDARDS - The term given to standards developed by the American National Standards Institute *(see entry).* Such standards are developed under democratic procedures whereby parties affected by the standards reach a consensus on their provisions. There are currently over 8,500 technically sound American National Standards which do not conflict with other national standards. *See International Standards Organization*

AMERICAN NATIONAL STANDARDS INSTITUTE (ANSI) - An organization founded in 1918 with the goal of ending "waste, duplication and conflict in voluntary standards activities, and user confusion about the acceptability of standards." ANSI coordinates voluntary standards activities in the U.S., approves American National Standards, and serves as the U.S. member of the International Standards Organization *(see entry)* and the International Electrotechnical Commission. *See American National Standards*

ANDEAN COMMUNITY - A customs union of Bolivia, Colombia, Ecuador, Peru, and Venezuela, created in March 1996 and scheduled for full implementation in 1999. The Andean Community is the successor to the Andean Pact created in 1969. Significant changes include the addition of a Secretary General, an elected Parliament, and a Court of Justice. The community is considering additional agreements, including a common market, free trade in services, and coordination of industrial policies.

ANDEAN PACT - *See Andean Community*

ANDEAN TRADE PREFERENCE ACT (ATPA) - A U.S. preferential program that took effect in 1991 under which the United States provides duty-free treatment to certain exports of Bolivia, Colombia, Ecuador, and Peru for a 10-year period. Articles which are eligible are the same as those under the Caribbean Basin Initiative *(see entry)* plus rum. The objective of the APTA is the expansion of constructive economic opportunities in the beneficiary countries.

ANNUAL REVIEW - A yearly update of antidumping and countervailing duty rates conducted by the Department of Commerce.

ANTICIRCUMVENTION - A provision of the Uruguay Round Agreements Act designed to deter circumvention of antidumping or countervailing duty orders. If a product is assembled or completed in the United States from parts or components produced in a country under an antidumping or countervailing duty order, the scope of the order may be expanded to cover those parts and components.

ANTIDUMPING ACT OF 1916 - *See Appendix IV*

ANTIDUMPING DUTY (AD) - A duty levied against entries of a product found to have been "dumped." This duty, sometimes levied retroactively, is equal to the difference between the producer's or exporter's sale price on the date of sale and the determined fair value of the product on the same date. *See Dumping, Agreement on Anti-dumping, Fair Value*

ANTITRUST POLICY - Government regulations designed to promote competition and thereby protect commerce and trade from monopolies and other restraints of trade.

APEC BUSINESS ADVISORY COUNCIL - A senior business advisory council to the Asian-Pacific Economic Forum, established in 1995 as a permanent body to succeed the Pacific Business Forum. Made up of two or three representatives from each APEC country, the council makes recommendations to APEC leaders on such matters as cross-border flows, finance and investment, infrastructure, and economic and technical cooperation. *See Asian-Pacific Economic Cooperation*

APPELLATE BODY - In the context of the World Trade Organization, a high-level group which is part of the dispute settlement mechanism. The Body hears appeals of decisions of panels. The Appellate Body is composed of seven members, three of whom serve on any one case. Members, appointed by the Dispute Settlement Board, are persons of recognized authority with expertise in law and international trade. They serve four-year terms.

APPLIED TARIFF RATE - The tariff rate actually used to determine the amount of duty owed on a particular import transaction. Applied rates may differ from bound rates. *See Bound Rates*

APPRECIATION - A strengthening or increase in the value of one currency when compared to another within a floating exchange rate regime. For example, if the U.S. dollar/German mark exchange rate has risen from $1.00=1.25 marks to $1.00=1.50 marks, then the U.S. dollar has appreciated against the mark. *See Depreciation*

ARAB MAGHREB UNION (UMA) - An organization of North African countries, established in 1989, with the aim of promoting cooperation and integration among the Arab states of northern Africa. The members are Algeria, Libya, Mauritania, Morocco, and Tunisia. *Syn. Maghreb Common Market*

ARCHITECTURE OF EUROPE - An informal term referring to the institutions, organizations, treaties, and customary relations that make up the European Union's sphere of operations. The Treaty on European Union establishes three pillars: first, the European Community; second, common foreign and security policy; and third, cooperation in the areas of justice and home (internal) affairs.

ARRANGEMENT REGARDING BOVINE MEAT - *See International Bovine Meat Agreement*

ASEAN FREE TRADE AREA - A free trade area involving the countries of the Association of South East Asian Nations (ASEAN) (*see entry*). Free trade within the region is scheduled to be phased in by the year 2003.

ASIAN DEVELOPMENT BANK (ADB) - An international development bank with headquarters in Manila, established in 1966 to promote investment, through loans and technical assistance, in developing countries in Asia and the Pacific region. The United States and most other industrialized countries are members of the ADB and provide its funds.

ASIAN-PACIFIC ECONOMIC COOPERATION (APEC) - An economic grouping of most countries of the Pacific rim, including Australia, Canada, China, Japan, Korea, Mexico, New Zealand, Taiwan, U.S., and the ASEAN nations (*see entry*). The group has met annually at the Heads of Government level since 1993 and has agreed to achieve free trade in the region by the year 2020.

ASSOCIATED PERSONS - *See Related Party*

ASSOCIATION OF CARIBBEAN STATES (ACS) - A grouping of 24 Caribbean countries, including Colombia, Costa Rica, Cuba, Dominican Republic, Guatemala, Honduras, Venezuela, and the members of CARICOM (*see entry*). The ACS has as its objective the promotion of trade, tourism, and transportation in the Caribbean region. *See Organization of Eastern Caribbean States*

ASSOCIATION OF SOUTH EAST ASIAN NATIONS (ASEAN) - A regional economic and political grouping established in 1967 to enhance cooperation among its member states - Brunei Darussalam, Indonesia, Laos, Malaysia, Myanmar, Philippines, Singapore, Thailand, and Vietnam.

AUSTRALIA-NEW ZEALAND CLOSER ECONOMIC RELATIONS TRADE AGREEMENT (ANZCERTA) - A free trade area between Australia and New Zealand, established in 1983. By 1990, all tariffs and quantitative restrictions on trade between the two countries were eliminated, as well as the application of antidumping duties. In addition, a number of non-tariff measures affecting the free flow of goods and services have been harmonized, including quarantine and customs matters, standards and business law. *See Closer Economic Relations*

AUTOMATED BROKER INTERFACE (ABI) - A component of the U.S. Customs Service's Automated Commercial System that permits qualified participants to file electronically import data required by Customs. ABI is a voluntary program available to brokers, importers, carriers, port authorities, and independent service centers.

AUTO PACT - Officially named the Automotive Products Trade Agreement (APTA) of 1963, this agreement provided duty-free passage between the United States and Canada of most automotive products . The Auto Pact was augmented by the 1988 Free Trade Agreement between the U.S. and Canada, which phased out the remaining auto duties over a 10-year period.

B

BALANCE OF CONCESSIONS - *See Concession, Reciprocity*

BALANCE OF PAYMENTS - The cumulative net result of all financial transactions of one country with the rest of the world. The major components are the current and capital accounts, along with the official settlements balance.

BALANCE OF PAYMENTS CONSULTATIONS - In the trade context, coordination between the WTO and the International Monetary Fund to ensure that where a country imposes trade restrictions for balance of payments reasons, the potential effects on other countries are taken fully into account. The WTO Understanding on Balance of Payments Provisions allows countries to deviate temporarily from their obligations if needed to remedy serious balance of payments problems.

BALANCE OF TRADE - The difference between a country's total imports and exports. When exports exceed imports, there is a trade surplus; the converse yields a trade deficit.

BARTER - *See Countertrade*

BASEL CONVENTION - An international agreement regulating the international movement of hazardous waste materials. The convention aims at preventing the export and import ofhazardous wastes in general. The signatories cooperate to achieve environmentally sound management of hazardous and other wastes. The convention was finalized in Basel, Switzerland, in 1989. Its formal name is "The Convention to Control Transboundary Movements of Hazardous Wastes and Their Disposal." The convention's signatories include 113 countries and the European Union. *Syn. Basel Agreement*

BASIC TELECOMMUNICATIONS SERVICES - The shorthand name of an agreement, effective in February 1998, concluded within the World Trade Organization to liberalize market access and national treatment in basic telecommunications. The agreement takes the form of a most-favored-nation protocol for those countries applying mutually beneficial, non-discriminatory access to foreign competition in basic telecommunications services. *Syn. WTO Basic Telecommunications Agreement*

BEGGAR-THY-NEIGHBOR POLICIES - A derisive term applied to policies, such as import restrictions, which address a country's economic problems in ways which harm the economies of other countries. The competitive escalation of tariffs after the stock market crash of 1929 is the classic example of such policies.

BENEFIT TO RECEPIENT STANDARD - A method for evaluating a particular subsidization by comparing it to any analogous commercial benefit(s) that would otherwise be available to the subsidy recipient within the jurisdiction in question. For example, if a government permits a tax deduction of $50 for each refrigerator manufactured in a depressed region, but a $75 deduction for each such refrigerator sold overseas, the "benefit to recipient" export subsidy is $25.

BENELUX UNION - A trade and customs union between the countries of Belgium, Netherlands, and Luxembourg, signed in 1944 and effective at the end of WWII. Belgium and Luxembourg have a full economic and monetary union (but with their own currencies), which was established in 1921. The three countries (along with the colonial possessions of Belgium and Netherlands) had established a Customs Union prior to the establishment of the GATT and, by virtue of a special provision in GATT Article I (section 2 (b)), were exempted from the normal GATT requirement that most-favored-nation treatment be extended to the other GATT members.

BERNE CONVENTION - Formalized in 1886 and now administered by the World Intellectual Property Organization *(see entry)*, the Berne Convention for the International Protection of Copyrights is founded on the concept of "national treatment" *(see entry)*. An author obtaining a copyright under the convention is given protection on the same terms as an author of the nation where protection is sought, and there is no discrimination against foreign nationals. The United States and 95 other countries currently adhere to the Berne Convention.

BICYCLE THEORY OF TRADE NEGOTIATIONS - The view that, unless forward momentum is maintained toward liberalization, the trading system will fall just as a stationary cyclist would.

BIG EMERGING MARKETS (BEMs) - A group of 12 economies identified on the basis of their sizable populations and rapid economic growth and development. The BEMs, with nearly half the world's population, are Argentina, Brazil, China, Hong Kong, India, Indonesia, Mexico, Poland, South Africa, South Korea, Taiwan and Turkey. The term was coined by the U.S. Department of Commerce as a means of attracting governmental and private sector attention to growth markets for U.S. trade and investment.

BILATERAL AGREEMENT - A formal or informal understanding between two countries.

BILATERAL INVESTMENT TREATY (BIT) - An agreement between two countries to guarantee the right of citizens of each to invest in the other on terms no less favorable than those accorded domestic or third-country investors. BITs commonly guarantee the free transfer of capital, profits, and royalties; freedom from performance requirements; access to international arbitration; and internationally recognized standards of expropriation and compensation. The United States has bilateral investment treaties with nearly all other countries.

BILL OF LADING - A shipowner's documentary receipt for goods accepted by a shipper of goods. A bill of lading serves not only as a receipt for the goods, but also as a contract of carriage and a document of title.

BINDING - The formal commitment of a country not to increase a given tariff. WTO Article II:1(b) provides that signatories may "bind" tariff rates by including them in schedules appended to the GATT. Once a duty is bound at a specific level, a signatory is free to lower it but may not raise it above that level without compensating affected parties. *See Bound Rates*

BLAIR HOUSE ACCORD - A bilateral agreement between the U.S. and EU to resolve agricultural trade issues. Concluded in November 1992, at the Blair House in Washington, DC, the accord removed some of the roadblocks to conclusion of the GATT Uruguay Round.

BLUE BOX MEASURE - A government program in the agricultural sector designed to promote agrilcultural and rural growth in developing countries. These measures take the form of direct payments to farmers who have been required by their government to restrict their output. Under Article VI of the WTO Agreement on Agriculture, "Blue Box Meaures" are excluded from the total Aggregate Measure of Support *(see entry)* that each WTO member must bind and reduce over time. *SeeGreen Box Measure*

BORDER TAX ADJUSTMENT - The remission, upon exportation, of taxes which have been paid on exported goods, so as to ensure that national tax systems do not impede exports. The WTO permits such frontier adjustments for indirect taxes, including sales taxes and value added taxes, which are passed on to consumers. The WTO does not sanction the remission of direct taxes (e.g., income taxes assessed on producing firms).

BOUND RATES - Most-favored-nation tariff rates *(see Most-Favored-Nation Treatment)* resulting from WTO negotiations and thereafter incorporated as integral provisions of a country's schedule of concessions. A bound rate may be the result of a negotiated reduction of a tariff rate, or may be simply a commitment not to raise an existing rate. If a WTO contracting party raises a tariff above its bound rate, the beneficiaries of the binding have a right under WTO to retaliate commensurately against the offending country's exports, or to receive compensation, usually in the form of reduced tariffs on products they export to the offending country. *See Binding*

BOUNTIES OR GRANTS - *See Export Subsidy, Countervailing Duties*

BOYCOTT - A refusal to deal commercially or otherwise with a person, firm, or country. In the 1970s, the trade boycott of Israel by a number of Arab and other countries led to U.S. legislation prohibiting U.S. firms from participating in that campaign.

BRETTON WOODS CONFERENCE - A meeting held under the auspices of the United States at Bretton Woods, New Hampshire in 1944, to set up cooperation in matters of international trade and payments for the post-World War II period. The International Bank for Reconstruction and Development *(see entry)* and the International Monetary Fund *(see entry)* were established at the conference.

BRUSSELS TARIFF NOMENCLATURE (BTN) - The international tariff classification system, formerly widely used, also known as the Customs Cooperation Council Nomenclature (CCCN). The BTN/CCCN has been replaced by the Harmonized System *(see entry)*.

BUFFER STOCKS - Commodity stockpiles designed to be used to moderate price fluctuations of the commodities involved. For example, goods from a stockpile may be sold when prices reach a predetermined ceiling level, and goods may be purchased to add to stocks when prices drop to a predetermined floor level.

BUILT-IN AGENDA - In the context of international trade, the fulfillment and timely implementation, through timetables and commitments, of the obligations and agreements of the General Agreement on Tariffs and Trade (GATT), as carried into the structures of the World Trade Organization (WTO).

BUREAU OF EXPORT ADMINISTRATION (BXA) - A unit of the U.S. Department of Commerce charged with implementing certain trade policies in the areas of national security, foreign policy, and short supply. BXA administers the Export Administration Act (EAA) by developing export control policies and by requiring and issuing export licenses for certain controlled commodities. Additionally, BXA enforces the EAA's antiboycott provisions.

BUSINESS AND INDUSTRY ADVISORY COMMITTEE (BIAC) - An advisory council of the Organization for Economic Cooperation and Development (OECD) *(see entry)* consisting of representatives of the business community of each member country. The U.S. representative on the BIAC is the U.S. Council for International Business, which is also the U.S. member of the International Chamber of Commerce.

BUSINESS PROPRIETARY INFORMATION (BPI) - In the context of antidumping and countervailing duty investigations, sensitive data on private companies' profits, investment, production processes, and sales patterns and practices. Such data may be disseminated only under an administrative protection order *(see entry)*.

BUY AMERICAN ACT - Enacted in 1933, a U.S. law mandating preferential treatment for American products in certain government procurement contracts. This act is waived for purchases covered by the Government Procurement Code. A number of the 50 states have enacted "Buy American" legislation for purchases made with state funds. *See Government Procurement Code*

C

C & F - A commercial term meaning cost and freight. Same as CIF, except that the value of a shipment expressed in C & F terms does not include the cost of transit insurance. *See Appendix VII*

CABOTAGE - In international shipping and transportation, the carriage of goods or persons between points within a single country.

CAIRNS GROUP - A group of 15 developed and developing country exporters (Argentina, Australia, Brazil, Canada, Chile, Colombia, Fiji, Hungary, Indonesia, Malaysia, New Zealand, Philippines, South Africa, Thailand, and Uruguay) whose common goal is to promote agricultural trade reform. Established in 1986, the Cairns Group meets regularly in Geneva and less frequently in various member countries (occasionally at the Ministerial level). The group takes its name from Cairns, Australia, the site of its first meeting.

CALL - In the context of a bilateral trade agreement which permits restrictions on bilateral trade in certain goods (notably textiles), a request for consultations by the importing country to the exporting country to discuss the establishment of a mutually agreed quota on a particular product or product category. A call can be issued if the importing country believes that its market is being disrupted or is in serious threat of being disrupted by the cited product. *See Quota*

CALVO DOCTRINE - The principle of international law which holds that jurisdiction in international investment disputes lies with the country in which the investment is located; thus, an investor has recourse only to the local courts. The principle, named after an Argentine jurist, has been applied throughout Latin America, and in other areas of the world.

CANADIAN INTERNATIONAL TRADE TRIBUNAL (CITT) - Established December 31, 1998, by subsection 3 (1) of the Canadian International Trade Tribunal Act, the CITT is an independent, quasi-judicial body formed out of the former Canadian Import Tribunal, the Tariff Board, and the Textile and Clothing Board. The CITT's responsibillities include: to investigate the existence of material injury, or threat thereof, from dumped or subsidized imports; to conduct "sunset reviews" *(see entry)* of antidumping and countervailing duty orders; to hear appeals of decisions from the Department of National Revenue made under the Special Import Measures Act (SIMA) *(see entry)*; to conduct inquiries on issues regarding government procurement, safeguards, and tariff relief for imported textile imports; and to advise the Minister of Finance on economic, trade, and tariff issues. The CITT is composed of nine full-time members, including a Chairman and two Vice-Chairs, who are appointed by the Governor of Council for a term of up to five years.

CAPITAL ACCOUNT - Together with the current account *(see entry)*, the capital account measures a country's balance of payments *(see entry)*. By definition, the two accounts must balance. The capital account includes net foreign lending, net foreign investment, and changes in currency reserves.

CARIBBEAN BASIN ECONOMIC RECOVERY ACT (CBERA) - U.S. legislation permitting non-reciprocal tariff preferences to developing countries in the Caribbean Basin area, to aid their economic development and to diversify and expand their production and exports.

CARIBBEAN BASIN INITIATIVE (CBI) - The program developed under the Caribbean Basin Economic Recovery Act of 1983 which allows the U.S. Government to grant unilateral and preferential trade and tax concessions to countries and territories of the Caribbean

Basin. While the CBI legislation permits duty-free importation of many goods, textile products, sugar, and certain other products are not covered by the program. CBI countries include Antigua and Barbuda, Aruba, Bahamas, Belize, British Virgin Islands, Costa Rica, Dominica, Dominican Republic, El Salvador, Grenada, Guatemala, Guyana, Haiti, Honduras, Jamaica, Montserrat, Netherlands Antilles, Nicaragua, Panama, St. Kitts and Nevis, St. Lucia, St. Vincent and the Grenadines, and Trinidad and Tobago.

CARIBBEAN ECONOMIC COMMUNITY (CARICOM) - The 14-member community composed of Antigua and Barbuda, Bahamas, Barbados, Belize, British Virgin Islands, Dominica, Grenada, Guyana, Jamaica, Montserrat, St. Kitts and Nevis, St. Lucia, St. Vincent and the Grenadines, Suriname, and Trinidad and Tobago, which formed an economic community in 1973. Its goal is to enhance the economic stability of its members by facilitating trade among them. CARICOM plans to have a common market in place by 1999.

CARIBCAN - A development-oriented trade agreement, under which Canada grants duty-free entry to qualifying goods from the countries of the Caribbean Commonwealth. For a product to be covered by this agreement, a minimum of 60% of the ex-works *(see entry)* price of the product must originate in any of the beneficiary countries or Canada. A number of goods sensitive to the Canadian economy are excluded, namely, textiles and clothing, footwear, luggage and handbag products, leather garments, lubrication oils, and methanol.

CARICOM - *See Caribbean Economic Community*

CARNETS - Customs documents issued under the terms of the "Admission Temporaire/Temporary Admission (ATA)," which permit the holder to carry or send sample merchandise temporarily into certain foreign countries without paying duties or posting bonds. Foreign customs regulations vary widely; in some countries, duties and extensive customs procedures on sample products may be avoided by obtaining an ATA Carnet. Under the ATA Convention, commercial and professional travelers may take commercial samples and related professional materials into member countries temporarily without paying customs duties and taxes or posting a bond at the border of each country visited. The carnets are generally valid for 12 months.

CARTEL - An organization of producers of a given item formed to regulate the production, pricing, or marketing practices of the organization's members in order to limit competition and maximize their market power.

CASH AGAINST DOCUMENTS (CAD) - A method of payment for goods by which documents transferring title are given to the buyer upon payment of cash to an intermediary.

CASH IN ADVANCE - A method of payment for goods by which the buyer pays the seller in advance of the shipment of goods. Usually employed when the goods are built to order, such as specialized machinery.

CASH WITH ORDER (CWO) - A means of payment by which the buyer pays cash when ordering; the order is binding on both seller and buyer.

CBI PARITY - A proposal to treat imports from the Caribbean Basin Initiative (CBI) *(see entry)* countries on the same preferential basis as imports from Mexico are treated under NAFTA.

CENTER FOR TRADE AND INVESTMENT SERVICES (CTIS) - An office within the U.S. Department of Commerce to promote increased participation of U.S. businesses in the economic development of countries receiving assistance from the Agency for International Development.

CENTRAL AFRICAN CUSTOMS AND ECONOMIC UNION - An arrangement dating from 1966 (revised in 1974) to promote a Central African Common Market with a common external tariff. Members include Cameroon, Central African Republic, Chad,

Congo, Equatorial Guinea, and Gabon. The Union's headquarters are in Bangui, Central African Republic.

CENTRAL AMERICAN COMMON MARKET (CACM) - A treaty, signed by Guatemala, El Salvador, and Nicaragua on June 3, 1961, with Honduras joining in 1962, for the purpose of unifying their economies and jointly promoting the development of Central America in order to improve the living conditions of its peoples. CACM Economic Ministers meet regularly, even when political meetings are ruled out by regional tensions. It is likely that the institutions of CACM may be revitalized through participation in revived Mexican economic growth and through a series of interlocking agreements with Latin American neighbors, the U.S., and the Caribbean. Plans are underway to include Panama and the Dominican Republic in the CACM.

CENTRAL EUROPEAN FREE TRADE AGREEMENT (CEFTA) - A free trade agreement between the Czech Republic, Hungary, Poland, Slovakia, and Slovenia. The main objective of this "Visegrad Group" is to create a free trade area within Central Europe as a first step in integrating CEFTA countries into Western Europe.

CERTIFICATE OF ORIGIN - A document attesting that goods were produced in a specific country.

CHAEBOL - Any one of approximately a dozen large Korean business conglomerates. These conglomerates are typically family-owned and controlled. Examples are Samsung, Hyundai, Daewoo, and LG. Pronounced *CHAY-bol.*

CHECK PRICE SYSTEM - A device sometimes used by Japan's Ministry of International Trade and Industry *(see entry)* to avoid charges of dumping in foreign markets by establishing floor prices for exporters.

CHINESE ECONOMIC AREA (CEA) - An informal term for the People's Republic of China (including Hong Kong) and Taiwan.

CIF - A commercial acronym standing for "cost, insurance, and freight." If the value of a shipment of goods is expressed in CIF terms, it includes all costs involved in shipping the goods from their port of embarkation to their port of destination. Other valuation systems include FAS and C&F. *See entries*

CLAYTON ACT - The 1914 antitrust law which deals with "probable" anticompetitive conduct. (This law built upon the Sherman Act *(see entry),* which only addressed completed anticompetitive acts.) The Clayton Act prohibits any type of discrimination against buyers on the part of a seller, through such means as lowered prices, commissions, or brokerage fees, and all other types of inducements, which are not made equally available to all buyers. Section 7 prohibits mergers or stock acquisitions which would significantly decrease competition or create a monopoly.

CLEAN FLOAT - The determination of an exchange rate by market forces alone, without government intervention or restrictions. *See Dirty Float*

CLOSER ECONOMIC RELATIONS (CER) - Another term describing the economic relations between Australia and New Zealand. *See ANZCERTA*

CODE OF CONDUCT - An international instrument that specifies acceptable international behavior by countries or multinational corporations. Several codes of conduct designed to "harmonize" the use of non-tariff trade measures were negotiated in the Tokyo Round of multilateral trade negotiations. GATT Articles III through XXIII contain commercial policy provisions that have sometimes been described as GATT's code of good conduct in trade matters.

CODE OF GOOD PRACTICE FOR THE PREPARATION, ADOPTION, AND APPLICATION OF STANDARDS - A WTO agreement consisting of a code of good practice for the preparation, adoption, and application of standards by central government bodies, plus provisions under which local governments and non-governmental bodies should frame and use technical regulations. The code requires that procedures for determining the conformity of products with national standards be fair and balanced, and that they not discriminate against foreign goods or in favor of domestic goods. In addition, the code encourages the mutual recognition of conformity assessments. To ensure that exporters worldwide can get access to all necessary information about technical regulations and standards as well as conformity assessment procedures, all WTO Members' governments are required to establish national inquiry points. *See Inquiry Point*

COLOMBO PLAN - An international agreement among 26 African states to promote their economic development in cooperation with Canada, the United Kingdom, and the United States.

COLUMN 1 RATES - In the U.S. tariff schedule, the tariff rates applicable to imports from countries that receive most-favored-nation treatment (MFN) from the U.S., or have normal-trade-relations (NTR) with the U.S. It is divided into two subcolumns, General and Special. General rates are the standard MFN/NTR rates, normally those "bound" under GATT comitments. Special rates are those arising from preferential programs such as the Generalized System of Preferences, or free-trade agreements such as NAFTA. *See Generalized System of Preferences, Most-Favored-Nation Treatment, Normal Trade Relations*

COLUMN 2 RATES - Generally, the tariff rates enacted by the Tariff Act of 1930 (the Smoot-Hawley Act). They are substantially higher than Column 1 Rates *(see entry)* and are currently assessed only on imports from the few countries not receiving MFN/NTR or even more preferential treatment from the U.S. *See Most-Favored Nation-Treatment, Normal Trade Relations*

COMECON - *See Council for Mutual Economic Assistance*

COMMERCE BUSINESS DAILY (CBD) - The U.S. Commerce Department's daily newspaper. CBD lists government procurement invitations and contract awards, foreign business opportunities, and foreign government procurements.

COMMERCIAL ACTIVITY REPORT (CAR) - An annual assessment prepared by each U.S. embassy on its host country's political, economic, and business activities. Also covered are the country's market potential, and strategies for increasing sales of U.S. products to the country.

COMMERCIAL CONTROL LIST (CCL) - A compilation of items whose exportation is subject to review and approval by the Bureau of Export Administration of the U.S. Department of Commerce. The list incorporates items controlled for reasons of national security, foreign policy, and short supply. The list is divided into 10 general categories: materials; materials processing; electronics; computers; telecommunications and cryptography; sensors; avionics and navigation; marine technology; propulsion systems and transportation equipment; and miscellaneous.

COMMERCIAL COUNTERFEITING - The practice of manufacturing or selling goods which defraud the purchaser by purporting to be produced by a manufacturer other than the actual manufacturer.

COMMERCIAL DEFENSE - A phrase, commonly applied by the European Union, to describe antidumping and countervailing laws and duties. *See Contingent Protection*

COMMERCIAL RISKS - In the context of payment guarantees of the U.S. Export - Import Bank, contingencies other than the political risks set out in the guarantee documents. Commercial risks include insolvency and protracted default. *See Political Risks*

COMMERCIAL TREATY - An agreement between two or more countries setting forth the conditions under which business between the countries may be transacted. A treaty may outline tariff privileges, restrictions or conditions of property ownership or use, the manner in which claims may be settled, etc.

COMMISSION ON INTERNATIONAL INVESTMENTS AND TRANSNATIONAL CORPORATIONS (CIITC) - A 48-member commission created by the United Nations Economic and Social Council in 1974. The CIITC and the UN Centre on Transnational Corporations *(see entry)* serve as focal points within the UN Secretariat for all matters related to transnational corporations.

COMMITTEE 113 (The 113 Committee of the EU) - A committee of national representatives of Member States of the European Union, established under Article 113 of the Treaty of Rome, which established the European Economic Community in 1957. The committee exists to assist the EC's executive body, now known as the EU Commission, in defining and implementing a common commercial policy, including tariff rates, export policy, and measures to liberalize or protect trade.

COMMITTEE ON AGRICULTURE (CTA) - The Standing Committee of the WTO which monitors and discusses trade in agricultural products.

COMMITTEE ON BALANCE OF PAYMENTS RESTRICTIONS - The Standing Committee of the WTO which authorizes, and then monitors, import restrictions which a country imposes on a temporary basis in order to address balance-of-payments problems.

COMMITTEE ON FOREIGN INVESTMENT IN THE UNITED STATES (CFIUS) - An inter-agency committee of the United States Government created in 1975 to monitor the impact of foreign investment in the United States. Until 1988, CFIUS operated as an informal working group. However, with the passage of the Exon-Florio Amendment to the Omnibus Trade and Competitiveness Act of 1988, CFIUS has been given the authority to review and recommend action against mergers, acquisitions, and takeovers that place U.S. assets under foreign control. CFIUS is chaired by the Treasury Department. *See Exon-Florio Amendment*

COMMITTEE FOR THE IMPLEMENTATION OF TEXTILE AGREEMENTS (CITA) - A U.S. Government committee, established by Presidential Executive Order 11651 on March 3, 1972, to supervise the implementation of textile bilateral agreements. Chaired by the Commerce Department, its members include officials of the State, Labor, and Treasury Departments, and the Chief Textile Negotiator of the U.S. Trade Representative's Office.

COMMITTEE ON REGIONAL ARRANGEMENTS (CRA) - A standing body of the World Trade Organization established to (1) examine the consistency of regional trade agreements with the rules of the WTO; (2) make recommendations regarding the required reporting on the operation of such agreements; and (3) evaluate the systemic implications of such agreements for the multilateral trading system.

COMMITTEE ON TARIFF CONCESSIONS - The Standing Committee of the WTO which reviews the results of tariff negotiations and oversees their implementation.

COMMITTEE ON TECHNICAL BARRIERS TO TRADE - A WTO committee established by the Agreement on Technical Barriers to Trade, composed of representatives from each party to the Agreement, to assist in consultations and in resolving disputes among parties on matters relating to the Agreement; and for such additional responsibilities as the parties assign to it.

COMMITTEE ON TRADE AND DEVELOPMENT (CTD) - A longstanding GATT body, now incorporated in the World Trade Organization, which examines questions of interest to developing countries and oversees the application of measures to further their development.

COMMITTEE ON TRADE AND THE ENVIRONMENT (CTE) - A standing body of the WTO concerned with relationships between trade, the environment, and sustainable development.

COMMITTEE TO STRENGTHEN U.S. TRADE LAWS (CSUSTL) - A private advocacy group composed of U.S. companies, individuals, and other groups concerned with promoting stronger trade laws and their vigorous enforcement. The agenda is largely defined by steel, textile, and semiconductor producer interests.

COMMODITIES - Broadly defined, any goods exchanged in trade. However, the term is usually used to refer to undifferentiated, widely traded raw materials and agricultural products that are traded principally on the basis of price. Such commodities are frequently traded through futures contracts.

COMMODITY AGREEMENT - An international understanding, formally accepted by both principal exporters and importers, regarding international trading of a raw material such as tin, rubber, or cocoa. Exporting countries often seek commodity agreements in order to boost prices; consuming countries are generally willing to agree to commodity agreements that seek solely to moderate extreme price fluctuations.

COMMODITY CREDIT CORPORATION (CCC) - An entity established within the U.S. Department of Agriculture in 1948, whose purposes are to stabilize, protect, and support farm income and prices; to assist in the maintenance of balanced and adequate supplies of agricultural commodities; and to facilitate the orderly distribution of those commodities. CCC activities have included purchases and sales of agricultural goods, and export subsidization.

COMMON AGRICULTURAL POLICY (CAP) - A set of policies and devices by which the Member States of the EU seek to merge their individual agricultural programs into a unified effort to "promote regional agricultural development, fair and rising standards of living for farm populations, increased agricultural productivity, and methods of dealing with security of food supply." Two of the principal elements of the CAP are variable import levies (tariffs) *(see entry)* and subsidies to promote exports of farm goods that cannot be sold within the EU at their high support prices.

COMMON EXTERNAL TARIFF (CXT) - The system of uniform tariff rates adopted by all members of a custom union.

COMMONWEALTH - An association of sovereign independent states to promote cooperation, consultation, and mutual assistance among members. The British Commonwealth, headquartered in London, is the most notable example, with over 50 member states. The principal unifying elements of the British Commonwealth are historic ties to England, and use of the English language. The United States is not a member.

COMMONWEALTH OF INDEPENDENT STATES (CIS) - A loose association of 12 republics of the former Soviet Union: Armenia, Azerbaijan, Belarus, Georgia, Kazakhstan, Kyrgystan, Moldova, Russian Federation, Tajikistan, Turkmenistan, Ukraine, and Uzbekistan.

COMMUNITY INTEREST - *See Public Interest*

COMPARATIVE ADVANTAGE - The trade theory concept, developed by David Ricardo, which says that two countries can engage in a mutually beneficial exchange of two products even if one country has absolute advantage in both goods, as long as each country exports the good it produces at a comparatively lower cost. *See Absolute Advantage*

COMPENSATION - Trade concessions, such as tariff reductions, intended to offset the damage caused to other trading partners by a country's trade restrictions. Under GATT Article XIX, any member country that raises a tariff above its bound rate or otherwise violates a trade concession without GATT justification must lower tariffs or make other concessions to offset the disadvantage suffered by its trading partners. If it does not, it may face offsetting actions ("retaliation") by affected parties. *See Retaliation*

COMPETITION POLICY - Phrase used outside of the U.S. that is the rough equivalent of U.S. antitrust policy (*see entry).*

COMPETITIVE NEED RESTRICTIONS - In the context of the Generalized System of Preferences for developing countries, measures which permit the withdrawal of tariff benefits on specified products from a country which has become a relatively efficient producer of those products.

COMPOUND TARIFF - A "mixed tariff" composed of a specific tariff plus an ad valorem tariff on the same imported item (e.g., $0.13/kg plus 5%).

COMPULSORY LICENSING - Authorization by a government for someone, without the consent of a patent owner, to make, use, or sell a patented product; use a patented process; or use, sell, or import a product made by a patented process. Compulsory licenses are granted by governments for many reasons, among them to permit local production if the patent owner is not manufacturing the patented product in that country.

COMPUTED VALUE - A method to establish the value of imported merchandise for customs purposes when it is not possible to determine the transaction or deductive value *(see entry)*. The sum of production costs and charges involved in preparing goods for export, plus the imputed profit and overhead, equals the computed value.

CONCESSION - In trade terms, a tariff reduction, a tariff binding, or some other measure to reduce import restrictions. Such concessions are usually accorded pursuant to negotiation and in return for concessions by other parties.

CONDITIONAL MOST-FAVORED-NATION TREATMENT - Most-favored-nation (MFN) treatment conditioned on the recipient's compliance with specific terms. All Members of the WTO, including the United States, accord unconditional MFN treatment to most other WTO Members. The United States, however, conditions MFN treatment for a limited number of countries, including China, on certification by the President that the country is in compliance with the

Jackson-Vanik Amendment to the Trade Act of 1974 (*see entry)*, or on a one-year waiver of those requirements.

CONFIRMED LETTER OF CREDIT (L/C) - A letter of credit underwritten, or backed, by a financial institution other than the issuer. An exporter who requires a confirmed letter of credit from a buyer is assured of payment by the second financial institution even if the buyer or the first financial institution defaults. *See Letter of Credit*

CONFORMITY ASSESSMENT - A generic phrase referring to the procedures for ensuring that a product or service meets its professed standards. It applies to the procedures used by governmental bodies to accredit laboratory certification bodies, the procedures used by those bodies to certify testing laboratories, and the procedures used by those labs to certify products.

CONSENSUS - In international organizations, sufficient support for a particular position to be deemed a decision of the body. Domestically, consensus can refer to agreement among a sufficient number of domestic interest groups to set objectives and to permit the carrying forward of a particular negotiating strategy. In either sense, consensus is distinct from unanimity and is often achieved by avoiding, rather than utilizing, voting.

CONSTRUCTED EXPORT PRICE - In the context of U.S. antidumping practice, the price at which imported merchandise is first sold (or agreed to be sold) in the U.S. to a purchaser not affiliated with the producer or exporter.

CONSTRUCTED VALUE - In the context of antidumping proceedings, one means of determining "normal value." It is the sum total of production costs, profits, and general and administrative selling expenses. "Normal value" may be "constructed" when a proper comparison cannot be made on the basis of home market or third country sales. *See Fair Value*

CONSULAR FORMALITIES AND DOCUMENTATION - Procedures that many countries - especially developing countries - require in connection with the importation of goods. For example, some countries require special invoices that must be approved by a government official as a condition of importation. These procedures often are impediments to trade.

CONSULTATIONS - Formal discussions among interested countries of any trade action by a GATT/WTO Member that may nullify or impair concessions made to another Member. Consultations may be requested under Articles XXII or XXIII of GATT. *See Impairment.*

CONSUMER SUBSIDY EQUIVALENT (CSE) - The percentage by which consumer prices are decreased on an item due to direct or indirect government support of its producers. *See Producer Subsidy Equivalent*

CONSUMPTION TAX - A levy imposed on the purchase of goods and services, rather than on income or savings.

CONTINGENT PROTECTION - A phrase, commonly used by Canadians, to refer to measures taken under the antidumping, countervailing duty and escape clause statutes that require a finding of injury. Some Canadians contend that the cost, intricacy, and uncertainty inherent in the U.S. quasi-judicial proceedings constitute a form of procedural protectionism.

CONTRACTING PARTIES (CPs) - The signatory countries to the GATT. When written entirely in the upper case, "CONTRACTING PARTIES" is used to denote the members collectively. Parties to the WTO are referred to as "Members," and any reference to contracting parties in GATT 94 should be read as "Members." GATT/WTO Members are now more commonly referred to as "Member States" or "Member Countries." *See Appendix II for list of Members*

COORDINATING COMMITTEE ON MULTILATERAL EXPORT CONTROLS (CoCom) - The 17-nation committee which monitored sensitive East-West trade, especially trade in high-technology products. The members were Australia, Belgium, Canada, Denmark, France, Germany, Greece, Italy, Japan, Luxembourg, Netherlands, Norway, Portugal, Spain, Turkey, United Kingdom, and United States. CoCom was abolished in March 1994.

COPYRIGHT - The exclusive statutory right of authors, composers, playwrights, artists, publishers, or distributors to publish and dispose of their works for a limited time. The variation in national standards and enforcement practices has led to increasing pressure for stronger and more uniform protection. *See Intellectual Property Rights, Berne Convention*

COREPER - Acronym (from French) for the Brussels-based committee of permanent representatives of the European Union's Member States. COREPER actually operates as two groups: COREPER 2 deals with foreign affairs, and COREPER 1 deals with other matters.

COST OF PRODUCTION - In antidumping usage, the fully allocated costs of producing a good. If there are inadequate sales in the home market at or above the cost of production, investigating authorities may use "constructed value" to determine "normal value." *(See entries)*

COUNCIL FOR MUTUAL ECONOMIC ASSISTANCE (COMECON) - Formed in 1949, COMECON was the Soviet-led economic community of Communist-ruled nations. Members were Bulgaria, Cuba, Czechoslovakia, German Democratic Republic, Hungary, Mongolia, Poland, Romania, Soviet Union, and Vietnam. Angola, Ethiopia, Laos, Nicaragua, and Yemen were observers. COMECON was dissolved January 1, 1991.

COUNCIL FOR TRADE IN GOODS (CTG) - A WTO body responsible for the functioning of the Multilateral Trade Agreements in Annex 1A of the WTO Agreement *(see Appendix I)*. It oversees the activities of eleven committees, the Textiles Monitoring Body, the Working Party on Notifications, and the Working Party on State Trading.

COUNTERFEITING – Trading in goods that are falsely marked as to their manufacturers. Counterfeit goods may be denied entry into a country.

COUNTERPURCHASE - A common form of countertrade in which an exporter in one country agrees to purchase a quantity of goods from another country in exchange for that country's purchase of the exporter's product. The goods being sold by each party are typically unrelated but are normally equivalent in value. *See Countertrade*

COUNTERTRADE - Transactions in which parties exchange goods without an exchange of cash. This practice, also referred to as barter, has become increasingly prevalent in trade with countries lacking significant reserves of convertible (hard) currencies. *See Counterpurchase, Offset Requirements*

COUNTERVAILABLE SUBSIDY – Any subsidy that is not deemed to be nonactionable under Article 8 of the WTO Agreement on Subsidies and Countervailing Measures. WTO/GATT rules authorize Members to apply countervailing duties if such subsidies cause or threaten material injury to a domestic industry. *See Actionable Subsidy, Prohibited Subsidy, Specific Subsidy*

COUNTERVAILING DUTIES (CVDs) - Duties levied on imported goods to offset subsidies to producers or exporters of those goods. Under the WTO Agreement on Subsidies and Countervailing Measures such duties may be imposed if the subsidy causes or threatens material injury. The duty is designed to nullify the injurious effects of the subsidy, permitting competition to continue on a fair basis. *See Countervailable Subsidy, Agreement on Subsidies and Countervailing Measures*

COUNTRY OF ORIGIN - The country in which a given product is considered to have been manufactured. In the case of textiles and apparel, the country-of-origin designation is highly significant because quotas restrict the importation of goods from many countries. In 1996, the U.S. country-of-origin rules were revised and clarified, with these general results: yarn - where the yarn is spun; fabric - where the fabric is woven, knit or formed; apparel - where the product is sewn; made-ups, including home furnishings - where the product's fabric is formed, knit or woven. Country-of-origin rules have proliferated along with international agreements on sectorial trade, regional free trade, and programs granting preferential trade status. Harmonization of country-of-origin rules is therefore a continuing issue in international trade.

COURT OF INTERNATIONAL TRADE (CIT) - A specialized Federal court, seated in New York City, having jurisdiction over any civil action against the United States arising from any Federal laws relating to international trade. The court hears antidumping, product classification, and countervailing duty cases, as well as appeals of unfair trade practice cases from the United States International Trade Commission. The CIT was originally established under the U.S. Customs Court Act of 1980 to replace the former U.S. Customs Court and expand its jurisdiction. The court is empowered to hear cases arising at any port or place within the jurisdiction of the United States. CIT's nine judges are appointed for life by the President, subject to Senate confirmation.

COVERAGE - The extent of applicability of a trade action, agreement, or policy.

CRAWLING PEG SYSTEM - The informal, popular name for the frequent revision of a supposedly fixed currency exchange rate. A crawling peg is usually a series of devaluations, deemed necessary to adjust for rapid inflation. Between changes, the exchange rate for the currency remains fixed. *See Exchange Rate*

CREDIT TRANCHE POLICY - The International Monetary Fund's basic policy on the use of its general resources. Credit is made available in four "tranches," each equivalent to 25% of a member country's credit quota. "Tranche" is the French word for "slice."

CRITICAL CIRCUMSTANCES - In U.S. antidumping and countervailing duty practice, a determination that permits the retroactive suspension of liquidation *(see entry)* for unliquidated entries entered up to 90 days prior to the Commerce Department's preliminary determination *(see entry)*.

CROCODILE DUNDEE CLAUSE - A proposed arrangement under which a derivative holder of a copyright would be protected to the same degree as the original copyright holder regardless of whether the derivative holder obtained the copyright through purchase or license. For example, a licensed distributor of a motion picture would be accorded the same protection against copyright infringement as the producer of the film. The term owes its name to the film "Crocodile Dundee," whose producers sought protection of this type.

CROSS RETALIATION - A means of retaliating against unfair trade practices in one trade sector through action in another sector.

CULTURAL SOVEREIGNTY - A doctrine asserted by Canada and other countries to justify certain trade barriers as a means to protect their cultures from being overwhelmed by "pervasive" mass media (especially from the U.S.). This doctrine has been invoked by France to restrict English-language programming in French media.

CUMULATION - In trade remedy proceedings, especially antidumping and countervailing duty investigations, the practice of determining whether injury to a domestic industry has occurred, by adding together the market effects of imports from more than one country under investigation. Under the U.S. trade laws and the Uruguay Round agreements on antidumping and subsidies, very low levels of imports are not subject to cumulation unless they collectively account for over seven percent, or nine percent for developing countries, of total imports during the period of investigation. *See Negligible Imports*

CURRENT ACCOUNT - The measure of the balance of payments for a country or other economic unit (such as the European Union). The current account is the sum of a country's international trade in goods and services, plus private and official transfers of funds. By definition, a country's current account must be in balance with its capital account *(see entry)*; if a country runs a deficit in its current account, it must be made up through international borrowing or foreign investment (a net surplus in the capital account).

CUSTOMS CLASSIFICATION - A detailed categorization and coding system used by customs officials to determine the applicable tariff rate for a particular item.

CUSTOMS COOPERATION COUNCIL (CCC) - *See World Customs Organization*

CUSTOMS COOPERATION COUNCIL NOMENCLATURE (CCCN) - A system, also known as the Brussels Tariff Nomenclature (BTN), for classifying goods for customs purposes. It has been superseded by the Harmonized System *(see entry)*.

CUSTOMS MODERNIZATION ACT - A statute passed by the U.S. Congress in 1993, as part of the NAFTA implementing legislation, that reforms the administration of U.S. Customs law, placing increased responsibility on importers. Importers' obligations to determine their own liability for Customs duties are referred to as "informed compliance."

CUSTOMS UNION - Any group of nations that has agreed to eliminate tariffs on goods traded among members, while imposing common external tariffs on goods entering from outside the group. The European Union is the best-known example.

CUSTOMS VALUATION AGREEMENT - Formally known as the "Agreement on Implementation of Article VII of the GATT 1994," this agreement provides detailed rules for the determination of value for customs purposes. These rules are designed to provide a fair, uniform, and neutral system of valuation based on transaction value, and to preclude the use of arbitrary or fictitious values. The agreement was first negotiated in the Tokyo Round and amended in the Uruguay Round. The agreement is monitored by the WTO Committee on Customs Valuation.

D

DAIRY EXPORT INCENTIVE PROGRAM (DEIP) - The DEIP, one of four subsidy programs operated by the U.S. Department of Agriculture (USDA), helps U.S. exporters meet prevailing world prices for selected dairy products in foreign markets. USDA pays cash to U.S. exporters, allowing them to sell their dairy products in targeted countries at prices below the exporters' costs of acquisition. DEIP is a classic example of an export subsidy, and has been vilified for several decades by the United States' trading partners, particularly low-cost dairy producers like Australia and New Zealand. DEIP's defenders say that it is necessary to help U.S. farmers meet competition from subsidizing countries.

D'AMATO PROVISION – *See Iran-Libya Sanctions Act (ILSA)*

DATE DRAFT - A financial obligation, like a check, which matures a specified number of days after issuance, without regard to the date of acceptance.

DAVIGNON PLAN - The European Communities' program for the modernization and restructuring of the steel industries of Member States. The program required a substantial reduction in EC steel-making capacity, principally through the closing of older plants. The EC provided financial help, particularly funds for payments to laid-off steel workers, to ease the transition. Production quotas, minimum prices, and import monitoring were used to stabilize supply and demand. Named for Etienne Davignon, the Belgian who devised the plan in 1978 while serving as EC Commissioner for Industry. All internal measures ended in 1990. Import restrictions, in the form of voluntary export restraint agreements with third countries, ended in 1992.

DEAD WEIGHT LOSS - The cost incurred to society when, by artificial means, the price mechanism is not permitted to work freely. In such cases, neither producers nor consumers benefit as much as the economy as a whole suffers.

DEBT/EQUITY SWAPS - The conversion of a foreign currency debt claim into an equity investment. Almost unheard of before 1982, debt/equity swaps became commonplace in Latin American countries with non-convertible currencies and large outstanding foreign currency debt. In practice, lenders holding a hard currency note sell it to the central bank of the debtor nation for local currency, which is then invested in the debtor country.

DECOUPLING OF AGRICULTURAL SUBSIDIES - A proposal advanced by the U.S. in the 1987 Uruguay Round negotiations as a solution to the problem of agricultural subsidies. It aimed at breaking the link between ("decoupling") government assistance to farmers and the farmers' decisions to produce or sell agricultural goods. Direct income supports and payments for maintenance of the agricultural ecology would be examples of decoupled assistance. Decoupling would render governmental assistance trade-neutral and thus permissible.

DEDUCTIVE VALUE METHOD - A means of determining value for the assessment of customs duties, set forth in the WTO Customs Valuation Agreement and in U.S. law. The deductive value method is used when more traditional methods (e.g., "transaction value") are not available or appropriate. The deductive value method calculates dutiable value by deducting certain costs and charges from the sale price to an "arm's length" buyer in the importing country market.

DEFICIENCY PAYMENTS - Payments which a government makes to farmers to compensate for all or part of the amount by which domestic market prices fall below government-set target prices for a commodity.

DEGRESSIVITY (DEGRESSION) - An American neologism referring to the characteristic of a trade restriction wherein the severity of the action diminishes over time. Examples: a tariff which decreases over the period in which it is in effect; a quota which increases during its lifetime.

DE MINIMIS MARGIN - A percentage of the value of a transaction which is deemed to be too small to have brought about or influenced the transaction.

In U.S.antidumping proceedings, the de minimis percentage is two percent in an investigation and 0.5 percent in an administrative review. In countervailing duty proceedings, the de minimis subsidy margin is one percent for most countries, but can be two or three percent for products of certain developing countries. In countervailing duty reviews, the de minimis margin is 0.5 percent. Under the WTO and U.S. law, de minimis margins are deemed unlikely to distort trade, and therefore are not to be offset by antidumping or countervailing duties.

In Canadian proceedings, the equivalent term is "insignificant." Canada uses the same standard for both initial investigations and administrative reviews: margins of two percent or less, in antidumping proceedings, and one percent or less, in countervailing duty proceedings, are deemed insignificant.

DEPOSIT OF ESTIMATED DUTIES - The element of U.S. antidumping practice which requires that provisional duties be deposited at the time of entry of merchandise covered by an antidumping duty order. The deposit is equal to the estimated dumping margin. *See Tariff Act of 1930*

DEPRECIATION - A decline in the purchasing power of a currency relative to one or more others as a result of market forces.

DEROGATION - An exemption from one part of an agreement granted to a country as an inducement for accepting the rest of the agreement.

DEVALUATION - A decline in the value of a currency vis-a-vis other currencies due to deliberate government actions.

DIFFERENTIAL AND MORE FAVORABLE TREATMENT - A paraphrase of "special and differential treatment."

DILLON ROUND - *See Appendix III: GATT Rounds, Item-by-Item Negotiations*

DIRTY FLOAT - A supposedly free-floating currency exchange rate which is actually manipulated by government intervention or restrictions to limit appreciation or depreciation; sometimes called a managed float. *See Clean Float*

DISCLOSURE MEETING - In U.S. antidumping practice, an informal meeting at which the Commerce Department's International Trade Administration discloses to parties to the proceeding the methodology used in an antidumping investigation or administrative review. A disclosure meeting is generally held promptly after the preliminary or final determinations of an investigation, or promptly after the preliminary or final results of a review. *See Tariff Act of 1930*

DISCRIMINATION - In the GATT/WTO context, disparate treatment of internationally-traded goods or services because of their sources or destinations. Members are generally prohibited from applying discriminatory treatment either to imports or exports. *See Most-Favored-Nation Treatment, National Treatment*

DISMISSAL OF PETITION - In U.S. antidumping practice, the termination of a proceeding based on a determination made by the Commerce Department's International Trade Administration that the initiating petition does not properly allege a basis on which antidumping duties may be imposed, does not contain supporting information reasonably available to the petitioner, or is not filed by an appropriate interested party. Dismissal is extremely rare. *See Tariff Act of 1930*

DISPUTE SETTLEMENT - The resolution (or the mechanisms for the resolution) of controversies arising from alleged violations of obligations by Members of the WTO or any other international agreement. In the GATT/WTO context, dispute settlement is governed by Articles XXII and XXIII of the GATT, and by the WTO Dispute Settlement Understanding (DSU). The DSU, for the first time, provides for binding dispute settlement findings that a member government may not block.

DISPUTE SETTLEMENT BODY (DSB) - The body established by the World Trade Organization's Dispute Settlement Understanding (DSU) to oversee the application of the DSU. All WTO Members are represented on the DSB. However, in cases involving a plurilateral agreement (*see entry*) only those governments party to that particular agreement may participate in DSB decisions. The understanding provides that each dispute is to be reviewed by a panel established for the purpose; the DSB must adopt all panel reports within 60 days, unless a party appeals or the DSB rejects the report by consensus (that is, without formal objection by any member country). *See DSU*

DISPUTE SETTLEMENT PANEL - A panel, normally consisting of three persons, established for the purpose of hearing a particular dispute among GATT/WTO Members. After considering submissions by the parties to the dispute, the panel submits a written report to the Dispute Settlement Body (DSB). The report contains a statement of the relevant facts, determines the applicability of relevant WTO agreements, and makes a recommendation as to the contested measure's conformity with those agreements.

DISPUTE SETTLEMENT UNDERSTANDING (DSU) - The "Understanding on Rules and Procedures Governing the Settlement of Disputes," adopted in the Uruguay Round. The DSU strengthens the dispute settlement procedures formerly in place under the GATT 1947. For instance, a party may no longer block adoption of a panel report on an alleged GATT violation. The DSU also establishes procedures for appeals of dispute settlement panel decisions, provides for implementation of panel decisions, and sets out the steps that may be taken in the event a Member fails to implement a panel decision.

DOMESTIC CONTENT LAW - The requirement that a certain percentage of the component parts of a product, or a certain percentage of the value of a product, be made in the country where the product is sold. In the 1980s, bills to require local content in automobiles sold in the United States were introduced in the U.S. Congress but were not enacted.

DOMESTIC INDUSTRY - In Canadian and U.S. trade law, the "producers as a whole of a domestic like product" *(see entry)* or those producers of a domestic like product whose output collectively represents a substantial proportion of the total domestic production of the product. Producers may be excluded from the definition of the domestic industry if they are related to an exporter or importer, or if they are found to be importing the subject good. *See Related Party*

DOMESTIC INTERNATIONAL SALES CORPORATION (DISC) - A corporation organized to take advantage of provisions under U.S. tax law wherein income from the export of U.S. products qualifies for substantial tax benefits. DISCs must be organized with a minimum capital of $2,500, and 95% of the DISC's assets and income must consist of qualified export assets and export receipts, as defined in U.S. tax law. A GATT panel determined that the DISC system constitutes a GATT-illegal export subsidy program because DISCs do not conform to generally accepted principles of offshore taxation. To give U.S. firms the benefit of a GATT-legal export incentive plan, Congress enacted legislation to permit the establishment of Foreign Sales Corporations *(see entry)*.

DOUBLE-COLUMN TARIFF - A tariff schedule listing two duty rates for some or all commodities. Imports may be taxed at a higher or lower rate depending upon the importing nation's trade relationship with the exporting nation. In the past, the United Kingdom maintained a double-column tariff to provide more favorable tariff treatment to members of the Commonwealth. The United States still maintains a double-column system. *See Column 1 Rates, Column 2 Rates*

DOWNSTREAM DUMPING - An indirect form of dumping which occurs when a foreign producer sells at below cost in its domestic market, that product is further processed, and the resulting good is sold to another country.

DRAWBACK - Repayment by the government, in whole or in part, of customs duties collected on imported merchandise when the merchandise is later exported, either in its original state or after subsequent manufacture into a different article. Drawbacks are sometimes provided when exported merchandise consists of, or incorporates, substituted domestic merchandise of the same quality and characteristics as the imported merchandise.

DUAL PRICING - The selling of identical products in different markets for different prices. This often constitutes dumping.

DUAL USE TECHNOLOGY - Technology used for both military and civilian purposes. The national security implications of dual use technology sometimes create difficult issues in the enforcement of the U.S. Export Administration Act.

DUMPING - In U.S. law and international agreements, the sale of a good for exportation at less than its "fair" or "normal" value. Fair or normal value is usually the price at which merchandise is sold for consumption in the domestic market of the exporting country, but may also be the export price to a third country, or a constructed value consisting of the fully-allocated cost of production plus profit and selling and administration costs. According to Section 731 of the Tariff Act of 1930 as amended, if the Department of Commerce determines that less-than-fair-value sales have occurred, and if the International Trade Commission finds evidence of material injury or the threat thereof, then an antidumping order will be issued, applying antidumping duties to subsequent imports of the merchandise found to have been sold at a price below normal value. This antidumping duty rate will be equivalent to the dumping margin, generally the difference between the normal value and the export price for the good. *See Agreement on Antidumping,, Dumping Margin, Export Price, Normal Value*

DUMPING MARGIN - The amount by which merchandise is sold in a foreign market below the home market price, a third country price, or the constructed value (its "fair value"). This margin is expressed as a percentage of the price in the importing country. To ensure a fair comparison between goods sold in the home (or third) market and for export, adjustments are made for differences in the merchandise, quantities sold, circumstances of sale, and level of trade. *See Tariff Act of 1930*

DUTIES COLLECTED - A measurement of trade based on the amount of money collected upon the importation of a particular commodity at a specified duty rate for a stated period of time. In international trade negotiations, the yardstick of "duties collected" may be used to assess the comparability of concessions between countries because it can provide at least a rough estimate of trade flows.

DUTY - A tariff *(see entry). See also Antidumping Duty, Countervailing Duty*

DUTY REMISSION - The refund or rebate of duties, or the full or partial exemption or deferral of duties. Drawback *(see entry)* is a form of duty remission. In a duty remission system, a company may import items into a country, process them there, and when the processed goods are later exported, receive a repayment of duties paid on the original imports. Duty remission in excess of the duties levied on the imported merchandise is considered an export subsidy.

DUTY SUSPENSION - A temporary, usually unilateral, waiver or reduction in tariffs. Duties are sometimes suspended to ease shortages of needed imports or to lower the cost of products not available domestically.

E

EAST-SOUTH TRADE - Trade between a non-market economy and a developing country.

EAST-WEST TRADE - Trade between a non-market economy and a developed market economy.

ECO-AUDIT - The review of a company's production and/or marketing methods with regard to their environmental impact. Eco-audits monitor such areas as waste reduction, energy efficiency, pollution (prevention), and plans for continued improvement of environmental performance. There is at present no protocol or convention on eco-auditing; eco-audits are performed on a voluntary, company-by-company basis. *See International Standards Organization.*

ECO-LABEL - A product mark to be awarded by the European Union to an EU producer who can show that its product is significantly less harmful to the environment than similar products. The EU environment ministers agreed to the concept of an eco-label in March 1992. The EU Commission and Member States are drafting proposals for eco-labeling criteria with the intention of stimulating supply of and demand for environment-friendly products.

ECONOMIC BULLETIN BOARD (EBB) - A computer website (http://www.ita.doc.gov/uscs/uscsebb.html)operated by the U.S. Department of Commerce to disseminate statistical information on the U.S. economy. *See Appendix VIII*

ECONOMIC NATIONALISM - The doctrine or policy of making a nation completely self-sufficient economically, so that it requires neither imports nor exports.

ECONOMIC POLICY COUNCIL (EPC) - *See National Economic Council (NEC)*

ECONOMIC RENT - The amount by which a producer's income exceeds his total operating cost and usual margin of profit. Economic rent is a windfall resulting from an artificial increase in price caused by a quota or other restriction of supply.

ECONOMIC SUMMIT - Traditionally, the annual meetings of the leaders of the G-7, the seven major industrial countries. Russia began attending the meetings in 1997, giving rise to the term G-8. *See G-7, G-8*

ECONOMIES IN TRANSITION - Countries attempting to replace centrally planned economies with market economies. Special transition rules apply to such countries under Article 29 of the WTO Agreement on Subsidies and Countervailing Measures *(see entry)*.

ECONOMIES OF SCALE - The reduction of per-unit production costs attributable to the advantages of larger, more concentrated production operations.

ECO-PACKAGING - The re-use and recycling of environmentally friendly product packaging.

ECU - *See European Currency Unit*

EFFECTIVE RATE OF PROTECTION - As distinct from the nominal rate of protection, the effective rate of protection is the percentage increase in the price of a product due to tariffs or other restrictions on imported inputs. The effective rate of protection is generally higher than the nominal rate. It depends greatly on the proportion of imported inputs used in production, but is extremely hard to determine accurately because many factors are usually involved.

EMBARGO - A restriction or prohibition on exports or imports, either with respect to specific products or specific countries. Historically, embargoes have most frequently been adjuncts to warfare, but they have also been established for reasons of politics, economics, or public health.

ENABLING CLAUSE - The clause in the Tokyo Round Framework Agreement which legalized the extension of preferences by developed GATT contracting parties to developing countries. *See Framework Agreement*

END-USER CERTIFICATE - A certificate issued by an importing country, certifying that a named party will be the end-user, or final consumer, in that country of merchandise to be exported from another country. Such a certificate is required by the United States to enforce export controls in any case where an export license is required for national security reasons. The requirement for end-user certificates is intended to assure that sensitive products are not delivered, through a middleman, to proscribed consumers in the importing country or third countries.

ENHANCED TELECOMMUNICATIONS SERVICES - Telecommunications transmission services to which there has been added a computer application of some kind, such as remote data processing, a data base service, internet access, voice mail, or protocol conversion. Enhanced telecommunications services may also be referred to as "value added" services or, less accurately, as "information services."

ENTERPRISE FOR THE AMERICAS INITIATIVE (EAI) - An international program inspired by the United States and launched in June 1990 to support development of a new economic relationship between the United States and Latin America. The EAI has trade, investment, debt, and environment aspects. Trade aspects include efforts to advance free trade agreements with Latin America and the Caribbean, particularly with groups of countries that have associated for purposes of trade liberalization.

ENTITIES - In the context of the WTO Agreement on Government Procurement, this term refers to government agencies, ministries, departments, and their subdivisions, as well as to state-protected monopolies and other para-statal organizations. Signatories agree not to discriminate against the products of other signatories in certain purchases of goods by those entities covered by the code. *See Government Procurement*

ENTRANCE FEE - In the context of the World Trade Organization, trade liberalization measures demanded of a prospective member as the price of admission to the WTO.

ENTRY SUMMARY - The documentation, usually on Customs Form 7501, required to complete a formal customs entry in the United States so as to enable the Customs Service to assess duties, collect statistics on imported merchandise, and determine whether other requirements of law or regulation are met.

ENVIRONMENTAL DUMPING - The practice of manufacturing goods without regard to the environmental effects of the production. By avoiding the costs of environmental protection, a producer may be able to offer his goods more cheaply than an international competitor who bears such costs. This is often seen as an unfair advantage akin to "dumping."

ESCAPE CLAUSE - A provision of the WTO that allows a country to suspend a tariff or other trade agreement concession when certain goods are imported in such increased quantities (absolute or relative to production) as to cause or threaten serious injury to competing domestic producers. In U.S. legislation, the "escape clause" provision for the taking of safeguard measures is Section 201 of the Trade Act of 1974. *See Safeguard*

EURO - The basic unit of the proposed single currency to be shared by the countries that join the European Monetary Union. Euro coins and bank notes are scheduled to be in full circulation by 2002. As of the start of 1999, 11 European nations had met the EMU's requirements for participation in the Euro system: Austria, Belgium, France, Finland, Germany, Ireland, Italy, Luxembourg, Netherlands, Portugal, and Spain.

EURODOLLAR - Terms used for U.S. dollars circulating in European banking markets. Some loans are made in Eurodollars. The future European currency "Euro" *(see entry)* will diminish the need for Eurodollars.

EUROPE 1992 - In 1985, the Heads of Government of the European Communities (EC, now the EU) Member States committed themselves to completing the establishment of a single European market by December 31, 1992. By that date the EC was to evolve into "an area without internal frontiers in which the free movement of goods, persons, services, and capital is ensured..." *See European Union, Appendix VI*

EUROPEAN ATOMIC ENERGY COMMUNITY (EURATOM) - Created by the Treaty of Rome in 1957, this community seeks to further the use of nuclear energy for peaceful purposes throughout the European Union. EURATOM is now run by the administrative structure of the EU.

EUROPEAN BANK FOR RECONSTRUCTION AND DEVELOPMENT (EBRD) - A multilateral development bank established in 1991 to assist countries in central and eastern Europe and the Commonwealth of Independent States *(see entry)* in their transition towards open-market economies. The EBRD focuses on promoting environmentally sound and sustainable long-term development by encouraging competition, privatization, entrepreneurship, financing, foreign direct investment and technical cooperation while working closely in cooperation with many other financial institutions. The EBRD maintains a membership of approximately 60 countries and currently operates in the following 26: Albania, Armenia, Azerbaijan, Belarus, Bosnia and Herzegovina, Bulgaria, Croatia, Czech Republic, Estonia, Former Yugoslav

Republic of Macedonia, Georgia, Hungary, Kazakhstan, Kyrgyzstan, Latvia, Lithuania, Moldova, Poland, Romania, Russian Federation, Slovak Republic, Slovenia, Tajikistan, Turkmenistan, Ukraine, and Uzbekistan.

EUROPEAN COAL AND STEEL COMMUNITY (ECSC) - The pool of steel-making resources established by Belgium, France, Italy, Luxembourg, Netherlands, and West Germany under the 1951 Treaty of Paris. The ECSC provided for the elimination of barriers to intra-ECSC trade in coal, iron, and steel, and permitted steel workers from any ECSC member country to work in the steel industry in any other member country. The ECSC was conceived in the wake of World War II by French statesman Jean Monnet, and formally proposed by French Foreign Minister Robert Schuman, in the hope of lessening the risk of future wars in Europe by breaking down national barriers that had protected these sectors and supported the military industry. The success of the ECSC led to the establishment of the European Economic Community in 1957. The ECSC Treaty is due to expire in 2002. *See European Communities, European Economic Community, European Union*

EUROPEAN COMMISSION - The Executive Branch of the European Union. As one of the five major institutions of the European Union, the Commission is responsible for ensuring the implementation of the Treaty of Rome, the Treaty of Paris, and EU rules and obligations; submission of proposals to the Council of Ministers; execution of the Council's decisions; reconciliation of disagreements among Council members; administration of EU policies, such as the Common Agricultural Policy and coal and steel policies; initiation of legal action against firms or member governments which the Commission finds in violation of EU competition policy (antitrust policy) or EU labor law or regulation; and representing the EU in trade and foreign policy negotiations with non-member countries.

EUROPEAN COMMUNITIES (EC) - The regional organization created in 1967 when, under a "treaty of fusion," the European Economic Community's institutions merged with those of the European Coal and Steel Community and Euratom *(see entries)*. The European Economic

Community was created by the 1957 Treaty of Rome, which established a customs union and looked toward other forms of political and economic cooperation. The treaty provided for the gradual elimination of customs duties and other intra-regional trade barriers; a common external tariff against other countries; and gradual adoption of other integrating measures, including a Common Agricultural Policy *(see entry)* and steps toward free movement of labor and capital. *See European Union*

EUROPEAN CURRENCY UNIT (ECU) - Prior to 1999, a constructed monetary unit whose value was determined by the value of a basket of currencies of Member States of the European Union. Originally used as a unit of account for EU budgetary purposes, the ECU also came to be increasingly used as the currency denomination for transactions within the European Community between companies, banks, and individuals. With the advent of the European Monetary Union on January 1, 1999, the single currency "euro" replaced the ECU.

EUROPEAN ECONOMIC COMMUNITY (EEC) - The customs union established by the Treaty of Rome on March 25, 1957, that provided for the free movement of goods among its member nations. Beyond a customs union, the treaty provided for common policies on agriculture, transport and competition; the harmonization of legislation; a social policy; and an external trade policy. The EEC's policy-making bodies, the Council and Commission, were merged with those of the ECSC and EURATOM in 1967 to form the European Communities (EC) *(see entries).*

EUROPEAN FREE TRADE ASSOCIATION (EFTA) - A regional trade grouping established in 1958 by the Treaty of Stockholm now comprising Iceland, Liechtenstein, Norway, and Switzerland. EFTA claims to have achieved nearly complete elimination of tariffs with respect to manufactured goods originating in member countries and traded among them. It is headquartered in Geneva. EFTA and the European Communities *(see entry)* have an agreement which provides for virtually free trade in most non-agricultural sectors.

EUROPEAN MONETARY SYSTEM (EMS) - A financial regime adopted by the European Communities (EC) in 1979. Its primary goal is to stabilize exchange rates among its Member Countries. The EMS has four major components: the euro *(see entry)*, an exchange and information mechanism, credit facilities, and transfer arrangements. The principal tool of the EMS is the Exchange Rate Mechanism (ERM)*(see entry)*. Under the ERM, the currency of each Member State is pegged to the euro and is allowed to fluctuate only within a narrow band (for most Member States, the band extends to 2.25% on each side of its established euro value). Member States are required to use central bank intervention when necessary to maintain the established parities.

EUROPEAN [OR ECONOMIC AND] MONETARY UNION (EMU) - The planned economic and monetary union of European Union members which will share a common currency (the "euro") and an independent central bank, the European Central Bank (ECB). What is to be the final stage of the EMU began on January 1, 1999 with the introduction of the euro. The Maastricht Treaty specifies budgetary and financial criteria that must be met by EU Members in order to be eligible to participate in the single currency arrangement. *See Euro*

EUROPEAN UNION (EU) - The body of nations created by and from the member states of the European Communiy under the 1991 Maastricht Treaty on European Union. The EU represents a broadening and deepening of the integration of the members of the European Community and is intended as a step toward even greater monetary and political integration. The EU's current 15 members are Austria, Belgium, Denmark, Finland, France, Germany, Greece, Ireland, Italy, Luxembourg, Netherlands, Portugal, Spain, Sweden, and United Kingdom. The structure of the EU is generally described as consisting of three pillars: (a) the European Communities, ultimately including a single currency and European citizenship; (b) a common foreign and security policy; and (c) cooperation among member states in the fields of justice and home (internal) affairs. *See Appendix VI*

EX WORKS (EXW) - At the factory door. Certain international transactions are concluded on the basis of ex-works prices (*see Appendix*

VII). In antidumping proceedings, adjustments to ex-works prices are often necessary to estimate comparable fair values for domestic and export sales.

EXCHANGE CONTROLS - The internal rationing of foreign currencies, bank drafts, and other financial paper to stabilize a country's balance of payments. Under exchange controls, an importer must obtain permission from his government to spend foreign currency. Exchange controls can distort trade and are often viewed as non-tariff barriers.

EXCHANGE RATE - The market price of one currency when purchased with another. For example, if one American dollar could be bought for 8 Hong Kong dollars, and vice versa, the exchange rate in U.S. dollars would be $1 U.S. = $8 HK, and in Hong Kong dollars $1HK=$0.125 U.S.

EXCHANGE RATE MECHANISM (ERM) - A program established in 1979 through which EU Member States agree to maintain parity in exchange rates among their currencies. Limits are set on the amounts by which exchange rates may vary between any two currencies. If an exchange rate reaches the limit, the central banks of the two countries intervene in the market to ensure that the limit is not exceeded. Disruptions in 1992 led to some parity realignments. Currency fluctuations of up to 15% were permitted as of early 1999.

EXCLUSIVE ECONOMIC ZONE (EEZ) - The 200-mile offshore area in which coastal states may control both the living and non-living resources of the sea, while allowing freedom of navigation to other states beyond 12 miles. The Exclusive Economic Zone gives the coastal states the responsibility for managing the conservation of all natural resources within the 200-mile limit. The EEZ concept was approved at the sixth session of the Third U.N. Conference on the Law of the Sea (UNCLOS) in 1994.

EXIMBANK - *See Export-Import Bank*

EXON-FLORIO AMENDMENT - An amendment to Section 721 of the Defense Production Act of 1950 by Section 5021 of the U.S. Omnibus Trade and Competitiveness Act of 1988 *(see Appendix I)* which empowers the President to investigate certain proposed acquisitions, mergers, and takeovers of U.S. companies by non-U.S. interests. If certain conditions are met, transactions that "threaten to impair the national security" may be blocked. President Reagan designated the inter-agency Committee on Foreign Investment in the United States (CFIUS) as the body with primary responsibility for implementing the Exon-Florio Amendment. *See Committee on Foreign Investment in the United States*

EXPEDITED REVIEW - In Canadian antidumping practice, a review of an outstanding antidumping order, undertaken at the request of exporters who have been uninvolved with any earlier phases of a case. *See 736 Review*

EXPORT ADMINISTRATION REVIEW BOARD (EARB) - A cabinet-level body of the U.S. Government established in 1970 to resolve disputes between federal agencies over export licensing. EARB membership includes the Departments of Commerce (as chair), State, Defense, and Energy; and the Arms Control and Disarmament Agency. Non-voting members are the Joint Chiefs of Staff and the Central Intelligence Agency. The EARB is the final review body to resolve differences among agencies on the granting of export licenses.

EXPORT-IMPORT BANK (EXIMBANK) - A U.S. Government-sponsored bank which provides guarantees of working capital loans for U.S. exporters, guarantees the repayment of loans, and makes loans to foreign purchasers of U.S. goods and services. The Export-Import Bank also issues credit insurance safeguarding U.S. exporters against the possibility of non-payment by foreign buyers for political or commercial reasons.

EXPORT PERFORMANCE REQUIREMENTS - Obligations which countries sometimes impose on foreign investors to export specified portions of goods produced as a result of the investments. *See Trade-Related Investment Measures*

EXPORT PRICE - In U.S. antidumping practice, the price at which merchandise is purchased or agreed to be purchased prior to the date of importation. The export price, after appropriate adjustments, is compared to normal value to determine the existence and magnitude of dumping margins. *See Constructed Export Price*

EXPORT PROCESSING ZONE - A type of free trade zone that promotes exports by using inducements such as reductions in taxes for certain export sales, and duty-free importation of equipment and raw materials used in the production of goods to be exported. *Syn. Special Economic Zones, Industrial Free Zones*

EXPORT QUOTAS - Specific restraints imposed by an exporting country on the quantity of a good which may be exported. Such restraints may be intended to protect domestic producers and consumers from temporary shortages of certain materials, or as a means to increase world prices of the commodities involved. *See Commodity Agreement, Orderly Marketing Agreement, Voluntary Restraint Agreement*

EXPORT RESTRAINT (ER) - A restriction placed by a country on its exports to a specified importing country. Usually, this results from a request (formal or informal) by the importing country. *See Voluntary Restraint Agreement*

EXPORT SUBSIDY - Any form of government payment or benefit given to an exporter or producer contingent upon the export of goods. Under the WTO Agreement on Subsidies and Countervailing Measures, subsidies, especially export subsidies, are recognized as measures which distort trade, unduly disturb the normal behavior of markets, and hinder GATT objectives. The Tokyo Round Agreement on Subsidies and Countervailing Measures prohibited, for the first time, export subsidies by developed countries on all non-agricultural goods. *See Subsidy, Subsidies Code*

EXPORT TRADING COMPANY ACT - *See Appendix IV*

EXTRAORDINARY CHALLENGE PROCEDURE - A procedure under the North American Free Trade Agreement (NAFTA) regarding panel reviews of antidumping and countervailing duty determinations, by which a NAFTA party may challenge a panel decision on the grounds that the decision was affected by (1) gross misconduct, bias, or conflict of interest on the part of a panel member; (2) the panel having departed from procedural rules; or (3) the panel having exceeded its powers, for example, by failing to apply the appropriate standard of review. Such challenges are decided by a committee of three judges selected by the parties.

EXTRATERRITORIALITY - The extension of the laws of one state to conduct and persons outside its territory, particularly where the conduct has no effect within the territory of the state concerned and the persons are not otherwise subject to its jurisdiction. The Helms-Burton Act *(see entry)* is considered by some U.S. trading partners as an improper extraterritorial statute.

F

FAIR TRADE - International commerce conducted without the benefit of dumping, subsidization, or the infringement of private rights such as trademarks. The 'fairness' of measures which affect trade varies according to the eye of the beholder.

FAIR USE - A long-standing doctrine of the U.S. copyright law, under which the fair use of a copyrighted work for purposes of criticism, comment, news reporting, teaching, scholarship, or research, is not an infringement of copyright. Whether or not a particular use will be considered a fair use depends upon a number of factors, including the nature of the work, the character of the use, the amount of the copyrighted work used, and the effect of the use on the market for the work.

FAIR VALUE - The U.S. antidumping statute authorizes the imposition of antidumping duties when foreign merchandise is being, or is likely to be, sold in the United States at less than fair value and imports of the merchandise concerned are causing or threatening material injury to a U.S. industry, or preventing establishment of a U.S. industry. Merchandise is sold at less than fair value when it is sold at less than "normal value." *See Normal Value*

FAS - A commercial acronym standing for "free along side." If the value of a shipment is expressed in FAS terms, it includes the cost of transportation to, but not onto, the vessel of exportation. In FAS contracts the seller pays the costs and assumes the risks of transporting contracted items to a position alongside the vessel or airplane of exportation. The seller is only required to deliver the goods to the designated loading area; the buyer is responsible from that point. *See Appendix VII*

FAST-TRACK NEGOTIATING AUTHORITY - The procedure, established for specific periods by statute, by which the U.S. Congress decides whether or not to implement a trade agreement or package of agreements concluded by the Executive Branch. Congressional action to approve or disapprove the legislative package submitted by the President is required within a specific time frame, without amendment. In practice, the Congress helps draft the legislation prior to its submission.

FASTENER QUALITY ACT - A law, enacted in 1990 and amended in 1996, designed to provide accurate information on industrial fasteners (e.g., bolts, screws) to the end user. The Act stipulates that certain fasteners must be produced according to the manufacturer's guidelines. This act regulates product inspection, testing, certification, and marking. The act is enforced by the National Institute of Standards and Technology, the Patent and Trademark Office, and the Commerce Department's Bureau of Export Administration.

FIFTH FREEDOM - In the context of international air travel, the right of an airline based in one country to pick up passengers from a second country and transport them to a third. Fifth freedom rights are sometimes referred to as "beyond rights."

FINAL DETERMINATION - In U.S. antidumping and countervailing duty practice, the conclusion of the second phase of the investigation of dumping or subsidies by the Department of Commerce and of injury by the U.S. International Trade Commission. If the Commerce Department final determination is negative, the proceeding is terminated. If it is affirmative, the USITC completes its investigation of injury by making a final determination. *See Preliminary Determination*

FINANCIAL SERVICES - Commercial services that relate to financing. The most important financial services in international trade are insurance and insurance-related services; and banking and other financial services, including brokerage transactions. The General Agreement on Trade in Services (GATS) deals with the particular intricacies and complexities related to financial services, and encourages additional market-opening commitments. *See General Agreement on Trade in Services*

FLORENCE AGREEMENT - Sponsored by the United Nations Educational, Scientific and Cultural Organization (UNESCO), the Florence Agreement was originally adopted in 1950 to provide for duty-free entry, under specified conditions, of various items which serve UNESCO's mandate "to facilitate the exchange of publications, objects of artistic and scientific interest, and other materials and information which promote the free flow of ideas." The Agreement has been amended to provide for duty-free treatment of certain equipment used in research, articles designed for handicapped persons, and other categories of special purpose goods.

FOB - A commercial acronym standing for "free on board." If the value of a shipment is expressed in FOB terms, it includes the cost of transportation to the port of exportation (or any other point specified), and the cost of loading the goods on a vessel, but does not include further shipment or insurance. Other valuation systems are CIF and FAS *(see entries)*. *See Appendix VII*

FOREIGN CORRUPT PRACTICES ACT - A 1977 Act of Congress making it illegal for a U.S. concern to promise or provide a thing of value to a foreign official or foreign political party as a means of obtaining or retaining business. Stiff fines and possible imprisonment up to five years are provided for such "corrupt" uses of influence as payments of cash and gifts. The FCPA contains several exceptions, including payments that are legal in the foreign country in question.

FOREIGN DIRECT INVESTMENT (FDI) - The acquisition by an investor based in one country (home country) of an asset in another country (host country). In most cases both the investor and its foreign asset are business firms. The investor is typically referred to as the "parent firm" and the asset as an "affiliate" or "subsidiary."

FOREIGN EXCHANGE BALANCING - A practice or policy that restricts a company's imports by limiting that company's access to foreign exchange with which to pay for them. Usually, the limitation is set at some proportion of the amount of foreign exchange earned by the company.

FOREIGN EXCHANGE CONTROLS - *See Exchange Controls*

FOREIGN MARKET VALUE - In U.S. antidumping practice, the price at which merchandise is sold, or offered for sale, in the principal markets of the country from which it is exported. If information on foreign home market sales is not usable, the foreign market value is based on prices of exports to third countries, or on constructed value. Adjustments for quantities sold, circumstances of sales, and differences in the merchandise can be made to those prices to ensure a proper comparison with the prices of goods exported to the United States. *See Tariff Act of 1930*

FOREIGN SALES CORPORATION (FSC) - An FSC is a non-U.S. corporation, organized by a U.S. producer or exporter in an eligible U.S. possession or in a qualifying foreign jurisdiction, which yields certain U.S. tax benefits on export sales. An FSC effectively exempts 15% of corporate export profits from the U.S. corporate tax; however, repatriated dividends are subject to U.S. taxation. Unlike a DISC (Domestic International Sales Corporation), an FSC is a foreign corporation and must have an offshore operation. *See Domestic International Sales Corporation*

FOREIGN SERVICE - The corps of American diplomatic and consular officials and support staff who serve to carry out U.S. foreign policy. Foreign Service functions include representing U.S. interests; operating U.S. overseas missions; assisting Americans abroad; public diplomacy; reporting; and negotiating on political, economic, consular, administrative, cultural, and commercial affairs. The Foreign Service is comprised of officers from the Departments of State, Commerce, and Agriculture; and from the United States Information Agency and the United States Agency for International Development.

FOREIGN TRADE ZONE - An area of a country where goods may be imported, stored, and/or processed without being subject to customs duties and taxes. Goods which enter the commerce of a country from the Foreign Trade Zone are subject to duties and taxes; goods which leave the zone and are then exported from the country are not. Also referred to as a "free zone," "free port," or "export processing zone."

FORMULA APPROACH - A method of negotiating tariff reductions using an agreed-upon formula applied to all tariff rates of all countries taking part. Limited exceptions may be provided for particularly sensitive items.

FOURTH WORLD - The world's poorest nations.

FOUR TIGERS - The Asian economies of the Republic of Korea, Hong Kong, Taiwan, and Singapore, whose rapid development led to the Asian economic boom of the 1980s and 1990s.

FRAMEWORK AGREEMENT - Internationally agreed principles drawn up pursuant to the Tokyo Declaration's call for consideration to be given to "improvements in the international framework for the conduct of world trade." Four separate subsidiary agreements make up what is known as the "framework agreement." They concern (l) differential and more favorable treatment for, and reciprocity and full participation by, developing countries in international trade; (2) trade measures taken for balance of payments reasons; (3) import restrictions imposed by less-developed countries for development purposes; and (4) an understanding on notification, consultation, dispute settlement, and surveillance in the GATT.

FREE LIST - A list of goods that have been designated as exempt from import duties or import licensing requirements in a given country.

FREE ON BOARD - *See FOB, Appendix VII*

FREE PORT - A port of entry into which foreign merchandise may be brought without being subject to the payment of customs duties. *See Foreign Trade Zone*

FREE RIDER - A country which, by virtue of the most-favored-nation clause, is the beneficiary of liberalizing action taken by other countries as part of a multilateral trade negotiation, but does not commit to equivalent liberalizing measures of its own.

FREE TRADE - A theoretical concept of international trade unhampered by governmental barriers such as tariffs or other restrictive measures. Free traders favor the reduction or elimination of tariff and non-tariff barriers.

FREE TRADE AGREEMENT (FTA) - An agreement between two or more countries to eliminate all, or substantially all, trade barriers between them. GATT Article XXIV prohibits countries which are participants in a free trade agreement from raising barriers to countries which are not parties to the agreement. The United States has free trade agreements with Canada, Israel, and Mexico. Other examples are EFTA, ASEAN, and MERCOSUR. *See North American Free Trade Agreement, U.S. - Israel Free Trade Agreement*

FREE TRADE AGREEMENT OF THE AMERICAS (FTAA) - The declared objective of countries in North and South America and the Caribbean to negotiate a free trade agreement encompassing the nations of the Western Hemisphere by 2005. It remains to be determined whether the FTAA will be negotiated from scratch, be an extension of NAFTA, or be a collage of provisions of the various existing regional agreements involving Latin American nations.

FREE TRADE AREA (FTA) - A cooperative arrangement among two or more countries to eliminate tariff barriers among themselves while not applying a uniform external tariff on imports from non-participating countries. The European Free Trade Association (EFTA) is the best known example of such an arrangement; others are the Latin American Free Trade Association (LAFTA) and the Association of Southeast Asian Nations (ASEAN) *(see entries)*.

FREE TRADE ZONE - *See Foreign Trade Area*

FUNCTIONING OF THE GATT SYSTEM (FOGS) - A Uruguay Round negotiating group whose purpose was to strengthen the GATT process itself. The group's goals were to improve GATT surveillance of trade policies and practices, to encourage greater involvement of trade ministers in the GATT, and to strengthen the GATT's relationship with other international organizations such as the International Monetary Fund.

FUTURES CONTRACTS - Contracts that allow for the sale of a commodity at specified prices to be delivered on a fixed date in the future. Futures contracts lock in prices and revenues for exports, thereby eliminating the risk of price changes before commodities are delivered. Exchange rate shifts, however, can bring about unanticipated losses and gains to those bound by futures contracts. Raw materials and agricultural products are typical of commodities traded in futures contracts. Futures contracts are sometimes called forward contracts.

G

G-3 - A grouping of three countries — Colombia, Mexico, and Venezuela — for the purpose of a mutual elimination of tariffs over a 10-year period. The agreement was reached on January 1, 1995 for a minimum of three years and is renewable for an indefinite period.

G-7 - The group of industrialized nations that participate in annual economic summit meetings. They are Canada, France, Germany, Italy, Japan, the United Kingdom, and the United States.

G-8 - The G-7 plus Russia, which was added as a participant in 1997.

G-10 - An informal group of developing countries which opposed the launching of the Uruguay Round. Led by Brazil and India, it included at various times Argentina, Cuba, Egypt, Nicaragua, Nigeria, Peru, Tanzania, and Yugoslavia.

G-15 - Established in 1990, the G-15 consists of relatively prosperous or large developing countries. The G-15 discusses the benefits of mutual cooperation in improving its members' international economic positions. Members include Algeria, Argentina, Brazil, Egypt, India, Indonesia, Jamaica, Malaysia, Mexico, Nigeria, Peru, Senegal, Venezuela, Yugoslavia, and Zimbabwe.

G-20 - A group of "moderate" developing countries which broke with the G-10 in the spring of 1986 paving the way to a consensus on concluding the Uruguay Round. Prominent roles were played by Colombia, Hong Kong, Jamaica, Malaysia, Mexico, Singapore, and Uruguay.

G-48 - The group of developed and developing countries that first endorsed an early draft of the Punta del Este Declaration in 1986. Most of the countries had been involved in the informal drafting sessions among the G-20 and the developed countries.

G-77 - Originally, a group of 77 developing countries which issued a joint statement in Geneva, Switzerland, in 1964. The G-77's primary function was to advance its members' collective interests, primarily in economic cooperation among developing countries and in negotiations on economic matters with developing countries. G-77 membership has increased to over 125 countries.

GAIATSU - Japanese for "foreign pressure." When the Japanese cannot resolve their differences internally, they sometimes welcome *gaiatsu.* Pronounced *gai-at-soo.*

GATT 1947 - The General Agreement on Tariffs and Trade (GATT) as negotiated after World War II and opened for signature on October 30, 1947, when 20 nations adhered. Its central objective was to develop "mutually satisfactory arrangements directed to the substantial reduction of tariffs and other barriers to trade...[and] to provide a forum" for settling disputes and for further liberalization of trade. As a result of the Uruguay Round, GATT 1947 was superceded by GATT 1994 and the World Trade Organization.

GATT 1994 - One of the principal components of the WTO system. GATT 1994 consolidates and combines most of the elements of the GATT system in effect from 1947 to 1994, plus new understandings on such matters as balance of payments and the Marrakesh Protocol to GATT 1994. *See Appendix I, Marrakesh Protocol*

GATT CODES OF CONDUCT- GATT instruments, negotiated during the Tokyo Round, which prescribed standards governing the use of non-tariff barriers to trade. Only the signatories of each code were bound by its terms. The nine codes were: Agreement on Technical Barriers to Trade (Standards Code); Agreement on Government Procurement; Agreement on the Interpretation and Application of

Articles VI, XVI, and XXIII (Subsidies Code); Agreement on Implementation of Article VII (Customs Valuation Code); Agreement on Import Licensing Procedures; Agreement on Implementation of Article VI (Anti-dumping Code); Arrangement Regarding Bovine Meat; International Dairy Arrangement; and Agreement on Trade in Civil Aircraft. *Syn. MTN Codes*

GATT/WTO PANEL - Under GATT-47, a board of neutral representatives established by the Secretariat at the direction of the Council to review the facts of a dispute, render findings of GATT law, and recommend action. *See Dispute Settlement Panel*

GATT ROUNDS - The eight sets of multilateral negotiations aimed at liberalizing trade, held under the auspices of the GATT from 1947 to 1994. *See Appendix III*

GATT WAIVER - *See Waiver*

GENERAL AGREEMENT ON TARIFFS AND TRADE (GATT) - A formal, multilateral agreement aimed at liberalizing and expanding world trade; or the organization that developed to administer it. The GATT was drafted in 1947 as an interim agreement pending establishment of the International Trade Organization (envisaged as the trade counterpart to the IMF and IBRD). The rules of the GATT provided specific disciplines over the use of trade barriers and helped reduce confusion and uncertainty in the international trade arena. The GATT also provided a forum in which countries could resolve trade disputes and negotiate progressive liberalization of tariff and non-tariff trade barriers. *See GATT 47, GATT 94*

GENERAL AGREEMENT ON TRADE IN SERVICES (GATS) - A multilateral agreement, negotiated as part of the Uruguay Round, which subjects trade in services to many, but not all, of the rules that apply to trade in goods. It is designed to promote more transparent laws and regulations affecting trade in services, to provide most-favored-nation treatment to foreign providers of services, to set up dispute settlement and enforcement procedures, and to provide for progressive liberalization through future trade negotiations. While Members are encouraged to accord national treatment to foreign producers of services, this is done only on the basis of specific commitments rather than as a general rule. *See Financial Services*

GENERAL COUNCIL (WTO) - Composed of all WTO Members, the General Council is the senior body responsible for the day-to-day work of the WTO. It oversees the activities of three other major bodies: the Council for Trade in Goods, the Council for Trade in Services, and the Council for Trade-Related Aspects of Intellectual Property Rights. The General Council also convenes as the Dispute Settlement Body and as the Trade Policy Review Body.

GENERALIZED SYSTEM OF PREFERENCES (GSP) - A system of developed-country tariff preferences in favor of the products of less developed countries, designed to encourage an increase of imports of manufactured and semi-manufactured goods from developing countries. The GATT and WTO have sanctioned this departure from the principle of nondiscrimination.

GENETICALLY MODIFIED ORGANISM (GMO) - In the context of food production, an organism whose genetic structure has been modified through biotechnology. Use of GMOs has caused considerable tension in U.S.-EU relations; American corn exporters have claimed that in 1998 EU restrictions on genetically altered corn cost them $200 million in lost exports. EU officials have sought to streamline the EU's procedures for approving GMOs, but several EU member states have suspended GMO approvals, and other member states have placed unilateral bans on GMO crops. The use of GMOs is likely to be a major issue in the Millenium Round of trade negoatiations.

GEPHARDT AMENDMENT - A proposed amendment to the 1988 U.S. Omnibus Trade and Competitiveness Act which sought to reorganize trade policy within the U.S. Government and centralize many trade policy matters in the Commerce Department. It also sought to force the U.S. Executive Branch to retaliate against "unfair" practices of U.S. trading partners. The amendment was defeated but helped pave the way for changes in Section 301, including the "super" and "special" 301 provisions. The amendment was proposed by 1988 U.S. Presidential candidate Richard Gephardt, a member of the House of Representatives from Missouri. *See Section 301*

GLOBAL ENVIRONMENTAL FACILITY (GEF) - An international program begun in 1990 to help developing countries protect the environment and to transfer environmentally benign technology to those nations. The facility focuses on four global environmental problems: climate change, pollution of international waters, destruction of biodiversity, and depletion of stratospheric ozone. It is jointly administered by the World Bank, the UN Environmental Program, and the UN Development Program.

GLOBAL FIRM - A firm which markets a product worldwide with little or no adaptation of the product, marketing strategies, or advertising. The Coca-Cola Company is an example of a global firm.

GLOBAL INFORMATION INFRASTRUCTURE COMMISSION (GIIC) - An international, non-governmental body established in July 1995 under an initiative by the Center for Strategic and International Studies (CSIS) to foster private sector leadership and private-public sector cooperation in the development of information networks and services, in order to advance global economic growth, education, and quality of life. The GIIC is an independent initiative involving 45 industry leaders from developing as well as industrialized countries. It was given a three-year mandate to pursue the following goals: (1) to strengthen the leadership role of the private sector in the development of a diverse, affordable, and accessible information infrastructure; (2) to promote involvement of developing countries in the building and utilization of truly global and open information infrastructures; and (3) to facilitate activities and identify policy options that foster effective applications of telecommunications, broadcasting, and information technologies and services.

GLOBAL QUOTAS - Limits set by one country on the total value or quantity of goods which may be imported from, or exported to, all other countries during a given period.

GLOBAL SOURCING COMPANIES - Firms that use imported goods or services as inputs for production in their home markets.

GOVERNMENT PROCUREMENT CODE - Formally known as the "Agreement on Government Procurement," this GATT Tokyo Round agreement provides that signatories will not discriminate against or among the products of other signatories in purchases covered by the code. The Agreement's coverage extends to purchases of goods (subject to exceptions) by specified government entities (e.g., ministries and departments) and specified para-statal enterprises listed in the Agreement, for all contracts valued over 150,000 Special Drawing Rights (SDRs) *(see entry)*. The WTO retained this agreement as a plurilateral agreement.

GOVERNMENT PROCUREMENT PREFERENCES - The purchase by official government agencies of goods and services furnished by domestic suppliers, despite their higher prices or inferior quality as compared to similar goods available from other countries.

GRADUATION - In the context of trade, the removal of a developing country from eligibility for special trade concessions such as those of the Generalized System of Preferences (GSP) *(see entry)*, based on its greater economic competitiveness and independence. "Graduated" countries are expected to assume the obligations of developed countries and to be more fully integrated into the trading system. For example, the Republic of Korea, Singapore, and Taiwan have been graduated from the U.S. GSP program.

GRANDFATHER CLAUSE - The provision of the GATT/WTO which allows signatories to maintain certain domestic legislation in effect at the time of their accession, even though it may be inconsistent with agreed rules. For example, upon accession to the WTO, the U.S. grandfathered the Jones Act (*see entry*). Although grandfathered provisions are theoretically expected to be brought into conformity with agreed rules as soon as possible, in practice they are accepted as long as their terms remain unchanged.

GRAY AREA MEASURES - Trade-restrictive actions, the legality of which is not clear under international trade rules. Gray area measures include voluntary restraint agreements (VRAs) and orderly marketing agreements (OMAs) *(see entries)*. The WTO provisions on safeguards were designed to eliminate gray area measures.

GRAY MARKET GOODS - Imported goods distributed through channels not authorized by the producer.

GRAY MARKET IMPORT - An imported product bearing a valid trademark but imported by a party other than the trademark holder or an authorized importer.

GREEN BOX MEASURE - A government program in the agricultural sector that has no, or only minimal, trade-distorting effects on production and does not have the effect of providing price support to producers. "Green Box Measures" such as government support for research, disease control, infrastructure, and food security are excluded from the total Aggregate Measure of Support *(see entry)* that each WTO Member must bind and reduce over time. *See Blue Box Measure*

GREEN SUBSIDY - *See Non-Actionable Subsidy*

GROSS DOMESTIC PRODUCT (GDP) - The total value of all the goods and services produced within a country in a given period (usually a year).

GROSS NATIONAL PRODUCT (GNP) - The total value of goods and services produced within a country plus the net value of any income earned abroad from either investment or work, during a specified period of time (generally a year).

GSM 102 and 103 - The most recent two in a series of programs of the U.S. Department of Agriculture for the purpose of granting export credits for U.S. agricultural exports. Both GSM 102 and 103 were provided for in the Food Security Act of 1985. GSM 102 is a short-term program offering up to three years of export credit; GSM 103 offers up to seven years of credit. GSM stands for "General Sales Manager."

GSP - *See Generalized System of Preferences*

GUARANTEED ACCESS LEVELS (GALs) - Guaranteed access to the United States market, at negotiated duty rates, for imported apparel or home furnishing products that contain both U.S.-manufactured and U.S.-cut fabric and that are sewn or assembled in one of the Caribbean Basin Initiative (CBI) countries or one of the nations of the Andean Pact. This access, provided for under the Caribbean Basin Special Access Program for Apparel, imposes duties only on the value added to the finished product, typically labor costs.

GULF COOPERATION COUNCIL (GCC) - A customs union of Persian Gulf nations, established in 1981 and headquartered in Riyadh, Saudi Arabia. The member states are Bahrain, Kuwait, Oman, Qatar, Saudi Arabia (the group's de facto leader), and the United Arab Emirates.

H

HABERLER REPORT- A report prepared in 1957 by a panel of experts led by Gottfried Haberler, a professor of economics at Harvard University. The report emphasized the need for attention to be given to agriculture and the developing countries in the GATT.

HAGUE CONVENTION - An agreement, formally known as the Convention for the Pacific Settlement of International Disputes, which created the Hague Permanent Court of Arbitration. The Convention was drawn up at two international conferences held in The Hague in 1899 and 1907, which have become known as the Hague Peace Conference. The Court of Arbitration has been inactive for several years.

HARD CURRENCY - A currency that may be exchanged for that of another nation without restriction. Sometimes referred to as convertible currency. Hard-currency countries typically have sizable exchange reserves.

HARMONIZATION OF TARIFFS - The reduction of a country's tariffs in a manner which makes the rates on various products more uniform. Most proposals for harmonization involve large cuts in high tariffs and smaller cuts in low tariffs. This approach contrasts with the "linear reduction" formula used in the GATT's Kennedy Round, which called for identical percentage cuts in tariffs. *See Appendix III*

HARMONIZATION FORMULA - An approach to tariff reduction wherein high tariff rates ("peak tariffs") are cut more, in percentage terms, than lower tariffs. The goal is to lower tariffs in a way which will achieve more consistent tariff levels among the negotiating partners.

HARMONIZED SYSTEM (HS) - An international system to classify traded goods according to standard six-digit codes. Beyond the six-digit breakdown, countries are free to introduce national distinctions for tariff or statistical purposes. The Harmonized System was implemented by several major trading nations on January 1, 1988, and the United States adopted it in the Omnibus Trade and Competitiveness Act of 1988, effective January 1, 1989.

HAVANA CHARTER - The post-World War II agreement which called for the establishment of the International Trade Organization (ITO) to oversee world trade. The ITO never came into force, largely because of opposition by the U.S. Congress. As a result, the General Agreement on Tariffs and Trade (GATT), which was negotiated at the same conference in Havana, evolved into the framework for multilateral trade, instead of the ITO.

HELMS-BURTON ACT - Drafted by Senator Jesse Helms (R- NC) and Rep. Dan Burton (R- IN), this law, also known as the Cuban Liberty and Democracy Solidarity (LIBERTAD) Act of 1996, formalized and expanded U.S. economic sanctions against Cuba. Its provisions include the right to deny U.S. visas to executives and majority shareholders (and their families) of companies that have invested in property that had belonged to U.S. companies prior to the communist revolution in Cuba. In July, 1996, President Clinton signed another provision of the Act that would allow American companies and individuals to sue in U.S. courts foreign companies benefiting from confiscated property in Cuba. As of early 1998, President Clinton had twice extended the date when that provision is to come into force. Trading partners of the U.S., notably Canada, the EU and Mexico, are strongly and vocally opposed to the Act.

HELSINKI ACCORD - A 1975 international agreement concerning the rights of people to travel freely. The tourism portions of the accord encourage (1) tourism studies; (2) preservation of artistic, historic, and cultural heritages of signatories; (3) lowering of fees and documentation needed for international travel; and (4) other efforts to encourage cooperation on tourism among countries. The U.S., Canada, and most European countries are signatories.

HIGH-INCOME COUNTRY - A World Bank classification. As of early 1998, any country which in 1995 had per capita gross national product (GNP) of at least $9,386. Typically, most high-income countries have industrial economies. There are an estimated 26 high-income countries in the world with a population of one million people or more. Their cumulative population is roughly 0.9 billion, less than one-sixth of the world's total population.

I

IMPAIRMENT - The GATT/WTO term for the harm to a country's trade interests caused by changes in the trade regime of another country, or by another country's failure to carry out its obligations under the agreement.

IMPERIAL PREFERENCE - A term referring to the special trade preferences and concessions which Article I of the GATT allowed countries to extend to their former colonies and dependencies. The WTO has no similar provision.

IMPORT LICENSE - A document attesting to the permission of a government for a person or firm to import specified goods.

IMPORT LICENSING CODE - Formally known as the "Agreement on Import Licensing Procedures," this Tokyo Round Agreement deals with the administration of import licensing systems. Incorporated in GATT 94, this agreement's purpose is to simplify and harmonize, to the greatest extent possible, the procedures that importers must follow in obtaining import licenses.

IMPORT QUOTA - A restriction on the amount of a particular commodity which may be imported into a country within a specified period of time. Import quotas may be "basket quotas," limiting total imports from all sources, or country-specific quotas, limiting imports from each exporting country individually. Some global quotas contain subquotas for specified supplier countries.

IMPORT QUOTA AUCTIONING - The process of allocating the right to import a good which is subject to an import quota by auctioning rights to import specific amounts of the merchandise.

IMPORT RELIEF - One of several terms (along with "safeguard action," etc.) used to describe measures imposed by the U.S. Government to temporarily restrict imports in order to prevent or remedy serious injury to domestic producers of the goods being restricted. *See Section 201, Appendix IV*

IMPORT RESTRICTIONS - Measures taken to control the level of imported goods. Common import restrictions are tariffs, import quotas, limits on the amount of foreign currency available to finance imports, import deposit requirements, import surcharges, and prohibitions of various categories of imports.

IMPORTS - In the context of American trade, commodities of foreign origin. For statistical purposes, imports are classified by type of transaction: merchandise entered for immediate consumption ("duty free" merchandise and merchandise on which duty is paid on arrival); merchandise withdrawn for consumption from Customs bonded warehouses and U.S. Foreign Trade Zones; and merchandise entered into Customs bonded warehouses and U.S. Foreign Trade Zones from foreign countries.

IMPORT SENSITIVITY - The vulnerability of domestic products to competition from imported products. *See Sensitive Products*

IMPORT SUBSTITUTION - The practice of encouraging domestic industries to produce goods previously imported. Import substitution programs are normally justified by the perceived need of the importing country to conserve foreign exchange and/or to spur economic development.

IMPORT SURCHARGE - A tax on imports over and above regular tariffs or customs fees. Import surcharges are sometimes imposed on a temporary basis by a country facing balance-of-payments problems. GATT Article XII permits such measures under certain conditions

INCOTERMS - A glossary, maintained by the International Chamber of Commerce (ICC), of terms used in foreign trade contracts to define the apportionment of costs in international transactions and to indicate at what specific point the costs are incurred by each party. *See Appendix VII*

INDIRECT TAX - A tax that is levied on commercial transactions rather than on income (e.g., a sales tax, excise tax, or value added tax).

INDIVIDUAL ACTION PLANS (IAPs) - Packages of trade liberalizing measures announced in November 1995 by members of the Asia-Pacific Economic Cooperation Forum *(see entry)*. These voluntary actions represented the first wide-ranging initiatives to expedite the implementation of APEC's Uruguay Round commitments and to deepen and broaden the outcome of the Uruguay Round through acceleration of tariff reductions, early implementation of WTO agreements, and deregulation.

INDUSTRIAL POLICY - Government programs designed to spur promising new industries, or to manage the decline of fading old ones. Mechanisms employed to encourage industry growth or rationalization include credit rationing, favorable access to investment funds and foreign exchange, the rationalization of cartels, joint research and development programs, control over licensing of technology, commercial policy (e.g. tariffs, quotas, export controls), and administrative "guidance" to the private sector.

INDUSTRY FUNCTIONAL ADVISORY COMMITTEE (IFACs) - A set of institutions established within the framework of the Industry Consultations Program for Trade Policy Matters, created by the Trade Act of 1974 and operated jointly by the Department of Commerce and USTR. There are three IFACs; they deal with customs matters, standards, and intellectual property rights.

INDUSTRY POLICY ADVISORY COMMITTEE (IPAC) - A private sector consultative body established in the context of the Industry Consultations Program for Trade Policy Matters, created by the Trade Act of 1974 and operated jointly by the U.S. Commerce Department and USTR. The IPAC is composed of leaders of U.S. industry who advise the U.S. Trade Representative *(see entry)* on broad policy issues in multilateral trade negotiations, pursuant to the mandate of the Trade and Tariff Act of 1984. *See Appendix IV*

INDUSTRY SECTOR ADVISORY COMMITTEES (ISACs) - Consultative bodies established under the Industry Consultations Program for Trade Policy Matters, created by the Trade Act of 1974. ISACs are committees of private sector representatives in each of the main industries, established to advise the U.S. Department of Commerce and the U.S. Trade Representative on trade negotiations. Although not mandated by statute until 1984, ISACs had been constituted as adjuncts to trade negotiations in earlier years.

INFANT INDUSTRY - A new, supposedly fragile area of economic activity. This term is used in connection with the idea that temporary protection in the form of tariff or non-tariff barriers can help establish an industry and enhance its eventual competitiveness in world markets. Although under the WTO a country may restrict trade to protect an infant industry, the country may be required to compensate adversely affected signatories. GATT Article XVIII outlines circumstances in which "infant industry" restrictions may legitimately be invoked.

INFORMATION TECHNOLOGY (IT) - The means for disseminating data, voice, and video information through computers, fiber optics, cellular, satellite, and other media.

INFORMATION TECHNOLOGY AGREEMENT (ITA) - An agreement reached in January 1995 by the U.S., Europe, and Japan, to a set of industry recommendations to the G-7 Meeting in Brussels on the Global Information Infrastructure (GII). The ITA, which took effect in July 1997, provides for the elimination of duties by the year 2000 on a variety of information technology products, such as multimedia personal computers, LAN equipment, supercomputers, and semiconductors. In 1998 talks began to expand the ITA to cover semiconductor manufacturing equipment, computer-based scientific and analytical equipment, and global positioning systems. Any new agreement is also expected to address non-tariff barriers.

INITIAL NEGOTIATING RIGHT (INR) - A right held by one WTO country to seek compensation from another WTO country for the impairment of a bound tariff. INRs stem from past negotiating concessions and allow the INR holder to seek compensation for an impairment of tariff concessions regardless of the holder's current status as a supplier of the product in question.

INJURY DETERMINATION - In U.S. law, a determination — sometimes referred to as a finding — by the U.S. International Trade Commission (USITC) *(see entry)* that imports are causing or threatening harm to a U.S. industry. These findings can also cover imports which retard the establishment of a domestic U.S. industry, although this provision is rarely invoked. Before trade restrictions may be imposed in a Section 201 case, there must be a finding that imports constitute, or threaten to become, a "substantial cause of serious injury." Injury findings are also required in anti-dumping (AD) and countervailing duty (CVD) cases *(see entries)*, in which the standard is "material injury," in conjunction with Commerce Department determinations on dumping and subsidization. However, in U.S. countervailing duty proceedings, the injury test is extended only to imports from countries that are WTO Members, have assumed obligations equivalent to the WTO Agreement on Subsidies and Countervailing Measures, or enjoy by treaty with the U.S. unconditional most-favored-nation treatment *(see entry)*.

INSIGNIFICANT - *See DeMinimis Margin*

INTEGRATION - With regard to international trade in textiles and apparel products, the removal of quantitative restraints (e.g., quotas) on imports during the 10-year phase-in of the World Trade Organization Agreement on Textiles and Clothing. Beginning in 1995, existing quantitative restrictions were to be removed from textile and apparel products in a series of steps, ending on January 1, 2004.

INTELLECTUAL PROPERTY RIGHTS (IPRs) - The right to possess, use, or dispose of intangible products of human ingenuity. International organizations such as the World Intellectual Property Organization *(see entry)* are dedicated to the protection of intellectual property by means of trademarks, patents, or copyrights.

INTER-AMERICAN DEVELOPMENT BANK (IDB) - The multilateral bank dedicated exclusively to providing resources for the economic and social development of Latin America and the Caribbean region. The IDB has two loan "windows." The first lends at near market terms, reflecting the cost of money in private capital markets. The second is the IDB's fund for special operations, which lends on concessional terms. Loans from this fund finance social development projects in such fields as health, education, and rural water supply. The United States and most other industrialized countries are members of the IDB, which has its headquarters in Washington, D.C.

INTER-AMERICAN INVESTMENT CORPORATION (IIC) - A multilateral investment corporation that promotes the economic development of its Western Hemisphere member countries by stimulating the establishment, expansion, and modernization of private enterprises, especially those of medium and small scale, in Latin America and the Caribbean. Affiliated with the Inter-American Development Bank, the IIC was established in 1986 and has its headquarters in Washington, D.C.

INTERGOVERNMENTAL CONFERENCE (IGC) - The formal mechanism for amending the Treaties of the European Union. Governments of the EU Member States meet to negotiate matters of major importance to European integration. In the history of the EU, there have been five intergovernmental conferences, three of which have convened since 1985. Significant results from IGCs have included the Single European Act and the Treaty on European Union. The fifth intergovernmental conference began with the Turin European Council in March 1996 and concluded with the Amsterdam European Council on June 18, 1997, resulting in the Treaty of Amsterdam. The fifth IGC addressed the challenges facing the EU in the new millennium, including further democratization of EU institutions, competitiveness and job creation, migratory pressures, and the future enlargement of the Union.

INTERNATIONAL BANK FOR RECONSTRUCTION AND DEVELOPMENT (IBRD) - Commonly referred to as the World Bank, the IBRD is an intergovernmental financial institution with the objective of raising living standards and promoting economic growth in developing countries. It grants loans to the governments of less developed member countries, or private enterprises in their territories, and stipulates that the funds loaned must be used to promote the long-term development of the countries. The IBRD generally lends only for specific development projects (i.e., agricultural and rural development, education, roads, and railways), and each loan must be guaranteed by the government concerned. The bank is headquartered in Washington, D.C. *See International Development Agency, International Finance Corporation*

INTERNATIONAL BOVINE MEAT AGREEMENT - An agreement in effect from January 1, 1980 to the end of 1997 that promoted the expansion, liberalization, and stability of international trade in meat and livestock, and fostered international cooperation in this sector. The agreement covered beef, veal, and live cattle. Since its termination, the former parties to the agreement rely upon information provided by national and intergovernmental bodies. The WTO Committees on Agriculture and on Sanitary and Phytosanitary Measures (*see entries*) now cover trade in meat and livestock.

INTERNATIONAL CHAMBER OF COMMERCE (ICC) - The world's largest business organization, with members in over 100 countries. The ICC promotes open and fair trade and seeks to facilitate the process of doing business internationally. It follows WTO affairs closely and makes recommendations to both the WTO secretariat and Member governments. The ICC has made an important contribution to the standardization of terminology used in international commercial transactions. In 1936, the ICC published a list of internationally recognized trade terms known as "Incoterms." This publication has since been revised a number of times; an edition was published in 1990. *See Appendix VII*

INTERNATIONAL COURT OF JUSTICE (ICJ) - Established in 1945, the ICJ is the principal judicial organ of the United Nations. The ICJ decides cases submitted to it by states and gives advisory opinions on legal questions submitted to it by the General Assembly or Security Council, or by UN specialized agencies. The court has 15 judges elected by the General Assembly and the Security Council from a list of persons nominated by the national groups in the Permanent Court of Arbitration. The seat of the Court is in The Hague, Netherlands.

INTERNATIONAL DAIRY AGREEMENT - An agreement which took effect January 1, 1980 and was terminated at the end of 1997, with the objective of expanding and liberalizing world trade in dairy products to achieve greater stability in the trade. In the interests of exporters and importers, it sought to avoid surpluses, shortages, and wide fluctuations in prices. The agreement aimed to assist the economic and social advancement of developing countries and to improve international cooperation in the dairy sector. The agreement, which was overseen by the International Dairy Council, covered all dairy products and allowed for agreed minimum export prices for international trade in certain milk powders, milk fat including butter, and certain cheeses. This plurilateral agreement was terminated due to "resource constraints faced by governments as well as the [GATT] Secretariat." The WTO Committees on Agriculture and on Sanitary and Phytosanitary Measures have taken on the responsibilities of the International Dairy Council.

INTERNATIONAL DEVELOPMENT AGENCY (IDA) - A part of the World Bank, the International Development Agency (IDA) lends funds to the poorest countries, usually at no interest but with a small service charge (three-fourths of one percent per annum), with repayment schedules of up to 50 years. Most of this IDA concessionary lending goes to Asian and African countries with extremely low per capita incomes. The funds for IDA come from budgetary contributions by more than 20 of the richer countries.

INTERNATIONAL EMERGENCY ECONOMIC POWERS ACT (IEEPA) - U.S. legislation, enacted in 1977, extending the emergency powers previously granted to the President by the 1917 Trading with the Enemy Act. The IEEPA enables the President, upon finding that a state of national emergency exists because of an external threat, to investigate, regulate, compel, or prohibit virtually any economic transaction involving property in which a foreign country or national has an interest.

INTERNATIONAL FINANCE CORPORATION (IFC) - The arm of the World Bank devoted to the development of the private sectors of the poorer countries. The IFC obtains its funds through stock subscriptions from member countries and from revolving loans and earnings. The function of the IFC is to encourage the flow of capital into private (rather than public) investments in developing countries. It makes loans at commercial interest rates, usually as a lender of last resort when the borrower cannot obtain sufficient capital from other sources on reasonable terms.

INTERNATIONAL FINANCIAL INSTITUTIONS (IFIs) - Organizations, funded by member nations, that lend money and/or expertise to developing nations. The IFIs include the International Bank for Reconstruction and Development (World Bank), the International Monetary Fund (IMF) *(see entries)*, and regional development banks including the Inter-American Development Bank, the Asian Development Bank, the African Development Bank, and the Arab Development Bank.

INTERNATIONAL LABOR ORGANIZATION (ILO) - An international group of governments and private associations of labor and employers, which seeks to promote improved working and living conditions by establishing standards in employment, wages, health, working conditions, and freedom of association among workers. Headquartered in Geneva, the ILO was founded in 1919 and became a special agency of the United Nations in 1946.

INTERNATIONAL MONETARY FUND (IMF) - An institution established in 1944 at the United Nations Monetary and Financial

Conference at Bretton Woods, New Hampshire to encourage international cooperation on monetary matters, including exchange rates and the payment of international debts. The IMF makes short-term loans to nations, both rich and poor, with balance-of-payments deficits, in concert with individual governments and private banks. The Fund's loan pool comes from contributions from member nations. In return for its financial help, the Fund imposes tight controls on a borrower's economy. Such controls include restrictions on government spending and on wage rates, in order to keep inflation down. The IMF has its headquarters in Washington, D.C.

INTERNATIONAL NATURAL RUBBER AGREEMENT (INRA) - The third of a series of international agreements concerning the production of, and trade in, natural rubber. Concluded in 1995 under the auspices of the United Nations Conference on Trade and Development (UNCTAD), the INRA offers a balance of benefits and responsibilities for consumers and producers of natural rubber. While maintaining most features of previous agreements reached in 1979 and 1987, the third INRA is more market-oriented than the previous ones. *Syn. INRA 1995*

INTERNATIONAL PRODUCT LIFE CYCLE - A life-cycle theory that explains trade flows along the following lines: an industrialized country exports a product, stimulating foreign competition; lower-cost foreign producers then begin to compete in foreign markets; and eventually foreign companies compete in the nation in which the product was originally produced.

INTERNATIONAL STANDARDS ORGANIZATION (ISO) – The ISO, founded in 1947, is the specialized international agency for product standardization. As of early 1999, it was composed of the national standards bodies of 100 countries. ISO promotes the development of standardization and related activities worldwide, with a view to facilitating international trade. For example, ISO developed the 9000 series of standards for quality management and quality assessment and the 1400 series for environmental management. ISO operates in all industrial sectors except the electrical and electronic engineering sectors, which are the responsibility of the International Electrotechnical Commission.

INTERNATIONAL TELECOMMUNICATIONS UNION (ITU) - A specialized agency of the United Nations responsible for developing operational procedures and technical standards for the radio frequency spectrum, satellite orbits, and the international public telephone and telegraph network. The Radio Regulations, resulting from ITU Conferences, have treaty status and spell out the principal guidelines for world telecommunications. The ITU has over 160 member nations and is located in Geneva, Switzerland.

INTERNATIONAL TRADE ADMINISTRATION (ITA) - A branch of the U.S. Department of Commerce which administers parts of U.S. antidumping and countervailing duty legislation and also supports the promotion and facilitation of trade. The ITA is composed of four principal units: U.S. and Foreign Commercial Service, Trade Development, Market Access and Compliance, and Import Administration.

INTERNATIONAL TRADE CENTRE - An agency, established by the GATT in 1964 and now operated jointly by the WTO and the United Nations Conference on Trade and Development *(see entries)*, which provides assistance to the export programs of developing countries.

INTERNATIONAL TRADE COMMISSION (ITC, or USITC) - An independent, quasi-judicial U.S. Government agency concerned with imports, import duties, and the effect of imports on U.S. industry. The USITC is charged with determining whether U.S. industries are materially injured by reason of imports that are dumped or subsidized. The Commission also makes recommendations to the President regarding relief for industries injured by increasing imports under Section 201 *(see entry)*. The USITC investigates unfair trade practices such as patent infringement under Section 337 *(see entry)* and may issue exclusionary orders *(see entry)*against infringing imports.

The Commission has six commissioners who are appointed by the President, confirmed by the Senate, and serve nine-year terms.

INTERNATIONAL TRADE ORGANIZATION (ITO) - A proposed body, conceived at the end of World War II as the trade counterpart to the IMF and IBRD *(see entries)*. The ITO never came into being, largely because of resistance in the U.S. *See Havana Charter, General Agreement on Tariffs and Trade*

INTERNATIONAL TROPICAL TIMBER AGREEMENT (ITTA) - An international accord intended to promote and facilitate trade in tropical timber while encouraging the sustainable utilization and conservation of the resource. The Agreement's objectives are furthered through special projects funded by consumer countries and conducted in producer countries. ITTA represents a partnership between the world's tropical timber exporters and importers for achieving the export of tropical timber from sustainably managed sources by the year 2000. The ITTA, negotiated in 1994, replaces a similar 1983 agreement.

INVESTMENT CANADA ACT - A Canadian law, enacted in 1985, intended to promote investment in Canada by Canadians and non-Canadians, and to establish review procedures of substantial non-Canadian investments in Canada to measure their net benefit to Canada. Generally, the responsible Canadian Government minister has 45 days to review such investments and determine if they are allowable. Should the minister decide that a potential or current investment will not, or does not, provide a sufficient overall benefit to Canada, then it will be rejected or terminated. This act replaced the Canadian Foreign Investment Review Act (FIRA).

INVISIBLES - The non-merchandise areas of trade -- freight, insurance, and most types of services and investment.

IRAN-LIBYA SANCTIONS ACT (ILSA) - Enacted as the "Iran and Libya Sanctions Act of 1996," legislation originally sponsored by Senator Alfonse D'Amato (R-N.Y.) requiring sanctions on non-U.S. companies that make investments of $40 million or more and significantly contribute to the development of Iranian or Libyan petroleum resources. This law's extraterritorial reach has been severely criticized outside the U.S. *See D'Amato Provision*

ITEM-BY-ITEM NEGOTIATION - A method of trade negotiations in which negotiators separately consider the probable trade effects of each proposed tariff cut. The intent is to ensure that, at the end of the negotiations, the total effect of cuts offered and received by each participating country will be in approximate balance. Early GATT negotiations followed this approach, but it became quite cumbersome by the time of the Dillon Round, leading to the linear reduction formula of the Kennedy Round. *See Appendix III, Dillon Round, Linear Reduction of Tariffs, Kennedy Round*

J

JACKSON-VANIK AMENDMENT - The common name for Section 406 of Title IV of the Trade Act of 1974 which established special rules for trade with non-market economy countries (NME's) other than those which were GATT members at the time the law took effect. Section 406 authorized the President to extend most-favored-nation treatment (MFN, now referred to as normal trade relations,NTR) to NME countries which undertook to reduce trade barriers and to loosen restrictions on the emigration of their citizens. The statute allows the President to waive the trade and emigration conditions for periods of a year; since 1980, China has been granted an unbroken succession of one-year waivers.

JAPAN EXTERNAL TRADE ORGANIZATION (JETRO) - Established in 1945 as a market research facility for Japanese industry, JETRO became a nationally chartered organization with an endowment from the Japanese Government in 1958. JETRO gathers commercial intelligence, conducts client-tailored market research, and does public relations for Japanese industry worldwide. While nominally an independent public corporation, JETRO staffs its overseas offices almost exclusively with personnel from the Japanese Government's Ministry of International Trade and Industry *(see entry)* and effectively functions as an operating arm of the ministry.

JAPANESE MINISTRY OF INTERNATIONAL TRADE AND INDUSTRY (MITI) - The governmental body responsible for the international trade and many industrial policies of Japan. MITI's exceptionally broad responsibilities are reflected in the names of its bureaus: International Trade Policy; International Trade Administration (including trade finance and export insurance); Industrial Policy (including price policy); Industrial Location and Environmental Protection; Basic Industries; Machinery and Information; and Consumer Goods Industries. In addition, MITI has four "external bureaus:" National Resources and Energy Agency; Patent Agency; Small and Medium Enterprises Agency; and Industrial Science and Technology Agency. MITI also controls the Japanese External Trade Organization (JETRO) *(see entry)*.

J-CURVE - The graphic description of the probable trend in a country's trade balance after a devaluation or depreciation of its currency. For a brief period of time a country's trade balance will deteriorate modestly before improving by a far larger margin than the original loss.

J-LIST - A list, appended to the U.S. Tariff Act of 1930 *(see entry)*, of products that are exempted from the normal requirement that imported goods be marked to show country of origin. These products are required to be packaged in containers marked to indicate country of origin. The items are in general those which it would be difficult or impossible to mark. Included on the list are such items as cut flowers, eggs, and fish hooks.

JOINT COMMITTEE FOR INVESTMENT AND TRADE (JCIT) - A body established by the United States and Mexico in October 1990 to demonstrate U.S. and Mexican commitment to greater economic cooperation. The committee identifies trade and investment opportunities and coordinates trade promotion events.

JOINT VENTURE - A cooperative undertaking between two enterprises wishing to benefit from shared technology, capital, or expertise. This is the common form of organization when a market economy enterprise is seeking to do business in or with a non-market economy or economy in transition.

JONES ACT - The statute, originally passed in 1898 and later incorporated into the Merchant Marine Act of 1920 (46 USC 883), that requires vessels which carry goods or passengers between U.S. ports to be built and documented in the United States and to be owned and operated by U.S. citizens.

JUDICIAL REVIEW - In the context of international trade, a mechanism for parties in an unfair trade case to appeal an antidumping or countervailing duty determination to a court of law in the importing country.

K

KEIRETSU - Major industrial groups of Japan, known before World War II as *zaibatsu*. *Zaibatsu* were typically family-owned and controlled; after WWII, family members were replaced by professional managers. Three of the largest and best known are Mitsubishi, Mitsui, and Sumitomo. Pronounced *kay-ret-soo.*

KENNEDY ROUND - *See Appendix III*

KOREA TRADE PROMOTION CORPORATION (KOTRA) - A non-profit organization established by the Korean government in 1962 to promote foreign trade. The corporation serves as an import promotion center offering a variety of free services in trade, investment, and international economic cooperation. KOTRA, with headquarters in Seoul, has a network of domestic and overseas offices, including several in the United States.

KOREAN INTERNATIONAL TRADE ASSOCIATION (KITA) - A non-profit, private business organization of Korean companies, which provides information and services concerning trade both for members and for foreign businesses. KITA's headquarters are in Seoul. Formerly called Korean Foreign Trade Association (KFTA).

L

LABOR SECTOR ADVISORY COMMITTEE (LSAC) - A committee of private sector advisors, consisting of trade union representatives and other labor experts, which advises the Labor Department and the U.S. Trade Representative on U.S. trade policy matters.

LAISSEZ FAIRE - A French term which has come to represent the theory that a government should not interfere with economic matters but should instead allow market forces to determine productivity and wealth.

LATIN AMERICAN FREE TRADE ASSOCIATION (LAFTA) - The original name of the Latin American Integration Association *(see entry)* when founded in 1960.

LATIN AMERICAN INTEGRATION ASSOCIATION (LAIA, ALADI) - A grouping ofLatin American countries established in 1980 to facilitate trade and economic development in the region. LAIA, or ALADI in Spanish, was formerly known as the Latin American Free Trade Association (LAFTA), which was founded in 1960. The members are Argentina, Bolivia, Brazil, Chile, Colombia, Ecuador, Mexico, Paraguay, Peru, Uruguay, and Venezuela.

LEAGUE OF ARAB STATES - A regional organization established in March 1945 for the purpose of improving relations among Arab nations. Members include Algeria, Bahrain, Djibouti, Egypt, Iraq, Jordan, Kuwait, Lebanon, Libya, Mauritania, Morocco, Oman, Palestine, Qatar, Saudi Arabia, Somalia, Sudan, Syria, Tunisia, United Arab

Emirates, and Yemen. Its headquarters are in Cairo. *Syn. Arab League*

LESS DEVELOPED COUNTRIES (LDCs) - The United Nations' term for "developing countries." There is no list of less developed countries that is accepted by all nations and international organizations, but the term generally includes all countries other than the members of the Organization for Economic Cooperation and Development and certain countries of Eastern Europe. Many people also exclude from this classification Israel, South Africa, and economies in transition *(see entry)*. The World Bank uses a tripartite system based on GNP per capita to classify the nations of the world. *See High-Income Country, Low-Income Country, Middle-Income Country*

LESS-THAN-FAIR-VALUE (LTFV) - Historical phrase used to describe sales of allegedly dumped products. "Fair value" has been replaced in usage by the term "normal value" *(see entry)*.

LESSER DUTY - The level of antidumping or countervailing duty sufficient to eliminate the injury to the domestic industry without fully offsetting the margin of dumping or subsidization. Under GATT/WTO rules, members are encouraged but not required to apply the lesser duty. U.S. practice has consistently rejected this approach.

LETTER OF CREDIT (L/C) - A written undertaking by a bank given to a seller at the request of a buyer to pay on sight or at a future date any amount up to a stated limit. The L/C is good for a specified period of time and is payable upon presentation of stipulated documents. The issuing bank substitutes its credit for that of the buyer. An L/C is used when an exporter does not want to rely on its overseas customer for payment.

LETTER OF CREDIT (Revocable) - A type of letter of credit which can be modified or canceled without the seller's consent, unless the letter has been transferred to a third party.

LETTER OF CREDIT (Revolving) - A letter of credit that includes a provision for reinstating its original face value after having been drawn down by partial payments. This kind of L/C facilitates the financing of on-going regular purchases.

LETTER OF CREDIT (Standby) - A letter of credit limited to the express purpose of effecting payment in the event of default by a debtor. The issuing bank is prepared to pay but does not expect to, and will not have to if the underlying transaction is properly completed.

LEUTWEILER REPORT - Published in March 1985 as "Trade Policies for a Better Future," the Leutweiler Report is a series of proposals presented by a group of eminent persons chaired by Dr. Fritz Leutweiler of Switzerland. The proposals called for "a new commitment to open trade, backed by improvements in the operation of the GATT system," and helped to identify the need for, and the agenda of, the Uruguay Round.

LIBERAL - When referring to trade policy, relatively free of controls or restraints.

LIBERALIZATION - Reductions in tariffs and other measures that restrict world trade. Trade liberalization has been the objective of all GATT/WTO trade negotiations.

LICENSING - As defined by the WTO Agreement on Import Licensing Procedures, the practice of requiring documentary approval for importation into a country. *See Import Licensing Code*

LIKE GOOD - *See Like Product*

LIKE PRODUCT - As defined in the WTO Agreement on the Implementation of Article VI *(see entry)*, like product refers to a product which is "identical, i.e. alike in all respects to the product under consideration, or in the absence of such a product, another product which, although not alike in all respects, has characteristics closely resembling those of the product under consideration." Canadian law refers to this international standard as "like good."

LINEAR REDUCTION OF TARIFFS - The reduction of tariffs by a given percentage on a whole range of goods. This is a far broader and simpler means of reducing tariffs than the item-by-item approach. *See Formula Approach*

LINER CODE - *See United Nations Code of Conduct for Liner Conferences*

LINER SHIPPING CONFERENCE - In maritime transportation, a group of shipping companies that jointly determine such matters as freight tariffs, sailing frequencies, and shipping capacity within a given geographic area.

LINKAGE - In the context of international trade negotiations, conditioning concessions in one area on offsetting concessions in another.

LOCAL CONTENT - The part of a product's value which is attributable to inputs originating in the home country. Many countries require that certain products marketed within their borders contain a specified percentage of local content; in the mid-1980s legislation to that effect was proposed (although defeated) in the United States for the automobile industry.

LOMBARD RATE - One of the official interest rates used by the German Government to regulate the money market and influence the national economy. Other countries use the term Lombard to describe rates that function somewhat like the Lombard rate. The Swiss, for example, have their own "Lombard" rate.

LOMÉ CONVENTION - Originally signed in 1975, this agreement, which replaced the Yaoundé Convention *(see entry)* with francophone countries, describes the European Union's financial and technical assistance programs to 71 "Associated Countries of Africa, the Caribbean and the Pacific " (ACP) *(see entry)*. In addition to giving certain preferential treatment to ACP products in the EU Market, the convention also produced a program known as STABEX *(see entry)* designed to stabilize earnings of the associated countries derived from the export of certain commodities. The Convention, which was renegotiated every five years after its inception until Lomé IV in 1990, is scheduled to expire in February 2000. At that time, the EU plans to negotiate a series of free-trade agreements to replace it.

LONDON INTERBANK OFFERED RATE (LIBOR) - The rate at which major London banks will lend one another Eurodollars. LIBOR is usually the average of rates for dollar deposits quoted by five major banks in the London market. Many international loan rates are tied to the LIBOR rate. A loan rate of LIBOR-plus-1 indicates that the borrower will pay variable interest at one percentage point over the current LIBOR.

LONDON INTERNATIONAL FINANCIAL FUTURES AND OPTIONS EXCHANGE (LIFFE) - Europe's leading exchange in futures contracts including short-term loans, government bonds, stock indices, and traded options on these instruments. The Exchange was established in 1982 to provide a means for hedging interest rates and currency exposures against volatility. Originally called the London International Financial Futures Exchange, LIFFE merged in March 1992 with the London Traded Options Market (LTOM) but retained its original acronym.

LONDON TRADED OPTIONS MARKET (LTOM) - *See London International Financial Futures and Options Exchange*

LONG-TERM AGREEMENT ON INTERNATIONAL TRADE IN COTTON TEXTILES (LTA) - The predecessor to the Multi-Fibre Arrangement Regarding International Trade in Textiles *(see entry)*.

LOUVRE ACCORD - An agreement reached in February 1987 by G-5 finance ministers and central bankers to use central bank intervention and monetary policy adjustments to keep the dollar within a narrow exchange rate range relative to the currencies of France, Germany, Great Britain, and Japan. The official communique made no mention of specific exchange rate ranges or targets; however, the range agreed to is commonly believed to be plus or minus three percent. *See Plaza Accord*

LOW-INCOME COUNTRY - A World Bank classification of poor nations. As of early 1998, any country which had a gross national product (GNP) per capita equivalent to $765 or less in 1995. Typically, most low-income countries have a low standard of living and few goods and services. There are an estimated 58 low-income countries in the world with populations of one million or more. Their cumulative population is approaching 3.2 billion.

LUSOPHONE COUNTRIES - Nations whose official language is Portuguese: Angola, Brazil, Cape Verde, Guinea-Bissau, Mozambique, Portugal, and Sao Tome and Principe.

M

MAASTRICHT TREATY - The treaty, in force since November 1993, which expanded the initiatives set forth in the Single European Act *(see entry)* and created the European Union. This treaty introduced a "three pillar" European Union, created European citizenship, and extended new authorities to the European Parliament according to the "co-decision procedure." The first pillar of the treaty revised and consolidated the three founding treaties: the European Coal and Steel Community, the ECSC; the European Atomic Energy Community, Euratom; and the European Community, EC *(see entries)*. The second pillar created a Common Foreign and Security Policy with provisions for collective action in foreign and security matters. The third pillar addressed issues relating to justice and domestic affairs such as immigration, asylum policy, and police cooperation with respect to certain areas (i.e. terrorism, transnational drug trafficking, and fraud).

MADRID ARRANGEMENT - The international framework of the Madrid system of international registration of marks. The arrangement provides for standardized international applications for, and registrations of, trademarks. This system is overseen by the International Bureau of the World Property Organization (WIPO) *(see entry)* and is managed according to two treaties: the Madrid Agreement Concerning the International Registration of Marks, 1891, and the Protocol Relating to the Madrid Agreement, 1996. The arrangement emanates from the Paris Convention *(see entry)*, but not all Paris Convention signatories are members of the Madrid Arrangement.

MADRID CONVENTION - *See Madrid Arrangement*

MAGHREB STATES - Generally, the three North African nations of Algeria, Morocco, and Tunisia. The European Union concluded a trade and aid agreement in 1976 with these states. The term sometimes also includes Libya and Mauritania. In 1989, the five Maghreb states created the Arab Maghreb Union *(see entry)*.

MANAGED FLOAT - *See Dirty Float*

MANAGED TRADE - Governmental influence on a country's trade. The influence is often indirect, such as through the government's industrial policies which affect the development and competitive position of certain industries.

MANUFACTURING CLAUSE - A provision ofUnited States trade legislation in effect from 1897 to 1986 which required that English language, non-dramatic, literary works by authors living in the United States be printed in the U.S. or Canada in order for the work to qualify for the full range of copyright infringement remedies. This provision was originally a temporary measure, but it was repeatedly extended. President Reagan vetoed a four-year extension of the law in 1982, but Congress overrode the veto. In 1984, a GATT panel found the provision to be in violation of the GATT, and Congress allowed it to expire in 1986.

MAQUILADORA SYSTEM - The widespread manufacturing system wherein components of U.S. origin (or which have been imported into the U.S.) are assembled in plants outside the United States (principally in Mexico, from whence the term comes), with the more finished product imported into the United States and subject to duty on only the value added in the assembly process.

MARGIN OF PREFERENCE - The difference between the duty that would be paid under a system of preferences and the duty payable on an MFN basis.

MARKET ACCESS - The opportunity for an industry to sell its products in a foreign country. Accessibility to a foreign market may be limited by tariff and non-tariff barriers to trade.

MARKET ACCESS COMMITTEE - The committee within the WTO Council for Trade in Goods which deals with market access issues among members. It is concerned with import and export practices that affect trade flows, such as tariffs and NTBs. The committee is developing a database on tariffs and trade.

MARKET DISRUPTION - The situation existing when a surge of imports of a given product into a particular country causes sales of domestically-produced goods to decline to such an extent that the domestic producers suffer major economic reversals. Under Section 406 of the Trade Act of 1974, the President may restrict imports into the United States from a communist country if the U.S. International Trade Commission finds "market disruption" due to the imports. The Act defines market disruption as "a significant cause of material injury or threat thereof," a much easier standard than "substantial cause of serious injury," which is the standard for action under the "escape clause" *(see entry)*.

MARKETING ORDERS - Mandatory directives issued by regional boards, established by the U.S. Department of Agriculture and including as members agricultural producers, as to the size and quality of fresh fruits and vegetables which may be marketed during specified periods within a given region. The boards draw criticism from time to time on the grounds that they keep prices high by limiting the kinds (and, consequently, the amounts) of produce which may be sold, and by setting standards that imported produce cannot meet.

MARKET ORIENTED, SECTOR-SPECIFIC (MOSS) TALKS -Talks held between the United States and Japan from 1985 to 1987 which sought to open Japanese markets in five key sectors. Several market-opening measures in the areas of telecommunications, medical equipment and pharmaceuticals, electronics, auto parts, and forest products were implemented as a result of these talks.

MARKET PROMOTION PROGRAM (MPP) - A United States Government export promotion scheme, authorized by the Food, Agriculture, Conservation, and Trade Act of 1990 and administered by the U.S. Department of Agriculture's Foreign Agricultural Service, under which surplus stocks or funds from the Commodity Credit Corporation are used to support agricultural organizations conducting specific foreign market development projects for eligible products in specified countries.

MARKS OF ORIGIN - The physical markings on a product that indicate where the article was produced. The United States and most other countries have customs rules requiring marks of origin. *See Rules of Origin*

MARRAKESH PROTOCOL - The accord of April 15, 1994, which established the World Trade Organization. It is included as a component of GATT 1994.

MATCHMAKER PROGRAM - A U.S. Department of Commerce program that assists small and medium-sized U.S. firms to establish business relationships abroad.

MATERIAL INJURY - *See Injury Determination*

MEMORANDUM OF UNDERSTANDING - An agreement signed by at least two nations usually providing for cooperation and joint action.

MERCANTILISM - A system by which a government regulates its economy so as to have a positive trade balance. The mercantilist economic philosophy equates the possession of gold or the accumulation of other international monetary assets, such as foreign currency reserves, with wealth. Mercantilist political leaders favor policies that promote exports and protect domestic industries competing with imports, on the theory that a trade surplus, which results in the accumulation of monetary assets, represents economic strength and possibly even moral virtue.

MERCOSUL - The Portugese acronym for "Mercosur".

MERCOSUR - Also referred to as the Southern Common Market, this is a regional trade agreement among Argentina, Brazil, Paraguay, and Uruguay. MERCOSUR entered into force in December 1994 under the Treaty of Asuncion. Modeled after the Treaty of Rome *(see entry)*, MERCOSUR established a common external tariff (CET); free movement of goods, services, and factors of production; a common trade policy regarding third nations; and coordination of macroeconomic and sectoral policies among the treaty signatories. The common external tariff was initiated January 1, 1995 in three phases: as of that date, a 20 percent CET limit was applied to 85 percent of all products, while tariffs on the remaining products will be limited to 14 percent for capital goods in 2001, and 16 percent for telecommunication and information technology in 2006. Chile has not sought entry to MERCOSUR, but does have an agreement with Argentina that accords it some similar benefits.

MIDDLE-INCOME COUNTRY - A World Bank classification. As of early 1998, any country which, in 1995, had had a gross national product (GNP) per capita of between $765 and $9,386. There are an estimated 67 middle-income countries with populations of one million or more. Their combined population exceeds 1.5 billion. *See High-Income Countries, Low-Income Countries*

MINIMUM VALUATION - The valuation for tariff purposes of all items below a certain value in an import category as if they were of that value.

MINISTERIAL DECLARATION - Before launching a round of Multilateral Trade Negotiations, trade ministers of GATT/WTO countries meet in special session to discuss whether to begin negotiations and, if so, the topics to be negotiated. Their decisions are set out in a Ministerial Declaration. GATT ministers met in special session in Punta del Este, Uruguay in September 1986 and decided to launch the Uruguay Round of multilateral trade negotiations. The Ministerial Declaration from this meeting set out specific objectives, the agenda for negotiations, and rules for participation. *See Punta del Este Declaration*

MITI - *See Japanese Ministry of International Trade and Industry*

MIXED TARIFF - *See Compound Tariff*

MODIFICATIONS - In the WTO context, alterations or withdrawals of tariff concessions. GATT Article XXVIII deals specifically with the modification of concession schedules.

MONTREAL PROTOCOL - A landmark international agreement designed to protect the stratospheric ozone layer. Originally signed in 1987 and substantially amended in 1990 and 1992, the protocol stipulates that the production and consumption of compounds that deplete ozone in the stratosphere, such as chlorofluorocarbons (CFCs), halons, carbon tetrachloride, and methyl chloroform, are to be phased out by 2000 (2005 for methyl chloroform). Signed by over 100 developed and developing countries, the Montreal Protocol also calls for a ban on the trade of controlled substances with non-signatory states. Developing countries which are parties to the agreement have an extra 10 years to meet the established control measures of the Protocol.

MOST-FAVORED-NATION (MFN) PROVISION - A promise in a treaty or agreement to extend to the other party or parties treatment at least as favorable as that granted to any other nation. *See Most-Favored-Nation Treatment*

MOST-FAVORED-NATION TREATMENT (MFN) - The granting, by one country to another, of the most favorable treatment accorded to any third country. When one country accords another most-favored-nation tariff status, it agrees to extend to that country tariff concessions at least as favorable as those it grants to any other MFN recipient. This concept may apply to non-tariff measures as well. WTO Members generally accord each other MFN status. Preferential treatment accorded to developing countries, and between members of customs unions and free trade areas, all represent allowable exceptions to the MFN principle. *See Appendix I, Normal Trade Relations*

MOTHERS-IN-LAW - A whimsical term used by EU Commission officials to refer to representatives of the fifteen Member States, to whom they are accountable.

MULTI-FIBRE ARRANGEMENT (MFA) - An international agreement in effect from 1974-1994 which allowed contracting parties to apply quotas on textile imports when importing countries considered them necessary to prevent market disruption. The MFA succeeded the Long-Term Agreement on International Trade in Cotton Textiles (LTA) *(see entry).* On January 1, 1995, the MFA was replaced by the WTO Agreement on Textiles and Clothing *(see entry).*

MULTILATERAL AGREEMENT - An international compact in which three or more parties participate.

MULTILATERAL AGREEMENT ON INVESTMENT (MAI) - The goal of a plan, agreed to in May 1995, for negotiations in the OECD aimed at developing agreed rules covering international investment. The proposed MAI would provide a broad multilateral framework for international investment, with high standards for the liberalization of investment regimes and investment protection, together with effective dispute settlement procedures. The MAI would be a free-standing international treaty open to all OECD Members and the European Union, and to accession by non-OECD Member countries, which would be consulted as the negotiations progressed. Negotiations for an MAI reached an impasse in October, 1998, and were broken off with no plan to be resumed.

MULTILATERAL ENVIRONMENTAL AGREEMENTS (MEAs) - Any agreement among countries based on the tenets that economic growth is essential for environmental preservation, and that protection of the environment is a fundamental condition of sustained growth. MEAs may provide for trade restrictions in order to protect the environment. Controversies arising from such trade restrictions are often subjected to WTO dispute settlement proceedings to assure their compliance with WTO rules and regulations. As of early 1999, there were more than twenty MEAs in existence.

MULTILATERAL INVESTMENT FUND (MIF) - A fund of the Inter-American Development Bank (IDB) *(see entry)* which provides program and project grants to facilitate investment reform and technical assistance for privatization in Latin America and the Caribbean, and to encourage domestic and foreign investment in the area. It was established in January, 1993.

MULTILATERAL INVESTMENT GUARANTEE AGENCY (MIGA) - An independent agency of the World Bank Group established by an international convention in April 1988. As of early 1998, it had 144 member countries — 124 developing countries and 20 industrialized nations. Its principal function is to guarantee eligible investments against non-commercial losses.

MULTILATERAL SPECIALTY STEEL AGREEMENT (MSSA) - A proposed international accord based on the Multilateral Steel Agreement (MSA) *(see entry)* and envisioned as a framework for trade in specialty steels. The MSSA was a narrower version of the proposed MSA that would have applied to high-value specialty steels only. Industry groups in the U.S. and the EU took the initiative in proposing the MSSA in 1996 but the proposal seemed to die when talks collapsed in 1997.

MULTILATERAL STEEL AGREEMENT (MSA) - A proposed agreement to eliminate tariffs, prohibit a broad range of non-tariff barriers (including certain anti-competitive practices), and ban, with a few limited exceptions, subsidies to steel producers. Formal negotiations began in 1990, but broke down in 1994. Subsequently, attempts were made by industry groups in the U.S. and Europe to restart the talks, but U.S. steel interests rejected a package of compromise proposals in late 1997, effectively killing the initiative.

MULTILATERAL TRADE NEGOTIATIONS (MTNs) - The eight rounds of negotiations held under GATT auspices since 1947. Each MTN has had the goal of reducing or eliminating tariffs among signatory countries; the Tokyo and Uruguay Rounds have focused on non-tariff measures as well. *See Appendix III*

MUNITIONS LIST, U.S. (USML) - A compilation of those items or categories of items considered by the United States Government to be defense articles or defense services subject to export controls. The USML contains some dual-use items whose exportation is controlled by the United States for national security and foreign policy reasons, and some items related to the nuclear field. The State Department, with the concurrence of the Department of Defense, designates articles to be controlled under the USML.

MUTUAL RECOGNITION - The process whereby two or more countries accept one another's standards and/or certification procedures for goods and services sold as industrial inputs or to the public as final products. The standards and/or certification can refer to product characteristics, such as the safety of an electrical appliance, or to the process by which the product was made, such as the use of large amounts of water without the pollution of waterways.

MUTUAL RECOGNITION AGREEMENT (MRA) - An international agreement covering standards in a particular product sector such as telecommunications, medical devices, pharmaceuticals, chemicals, or processed foods, under which countries accept each other's test results.

N

NAFTA DISPUTE SETTLEMENT - The dispute settlement mechanism established under the North American Free Trade Agreement (NAFTA), whereby a trilateral panel composed of representatives from the member countries (Canada, Mexico and the United States) adjudicates disputes over the interpretation of the NAFTA agreement. Dispute settlement panels deal with specific issues, such as the consistency of an antidumping determination with the law of the member country, or with broader issues, such as an interpretation of the NAFTA accord as it relates to the environmental obligations of each member.

NAFTA PARITY - A proposed U.S. policy to permit products originating in Caribbean countries to enter the United States at the same tariff rates as for Mexican and Canadian goods under NAFTA.

NATIONAL ECONOMIC COUNCIL (NEC) - A council created by President Clinton in 1993 to coordinate the decisions of the Federal Government's executive agencies in the area of economic affairs. The NEC is the economic policy equivalent of the National Security Council (NSC). The NEC replaced the Economic Policy Council.

NATIONAL TRADE ESTIMATES REPORT - An annual report to the U.S. Congress by the Office of the U.S. Trade Representative, providing an inventory of the most significant foreign barriers to U.S. exports of goods and services, and of barriers to U.S. investments and intellectual property rights.

NATIONAL TREATMENT - The GATT/WTO principle which requires that internal taxes apply equally to domestic and imported products, and that regulations treat imported goods "no less favorably" than similar domestic goods.

NATURAL RESOURCE-BASED PRODUCTS - Traditionally, forestry products, fishery products, and nonferrous metals and minerals, as well as derivatives of these products.

NEGLIGIBLE IMPORTS - In U.S. antidumping practice, imports from a country that accounts for less than 3 percent of the volume of all such merchandise imported in the most recent 12-month period. Negligible imports normally may not be cumulated for purposes of making an injury determination. *See Cumulation*

NEGOTIATING GROUPS - *See Uruguay Round Negotiations*

NET COUNTERVAILABLE SUBSIDY - In U.S. countervailing duty practice, the gross countervailable subsidy less (1) any application fee, deposit, or other payment made to qualify for or receive the subsidy; (2) any loss in value resulting from deferred receipt mandated by government order; and (3) export taxes and other charges levied on exports to the U.S. with the specific intent of offsetting the countervailable subsidy.

NET FOREIGN INVESTMENT - For the United States, the difference between the sum of U.S. imports of goods and services, receipts of factor income, and net capital grants received by the United States; and the sum of exports of goods and services by the United States, payments of factor income, and net transfer payments to foreigners. It may also be viewed as the total value of the acquisitions of foreign assets by U.S. residents, less total value of the acquisitions of U.S. assets by foreign residents.

NEWLY INDEPENDENT STATES (NIS) - *See Commonwealth of Independent States*

NEWLY INDUSTRIALIZING COUNTRIES (NICs) - Those developing countries which have reached a relatively advanced stage of economic growth and have experienced high growth rates in recent years. The NICs include Brazil, Hong Kong, the Republic of Korea, Singapore, and Taiwan. In some formal usages, the term NICs has been replaced by Newly Industrialized Economies *(see entry).*

NEWLY INDUSTRIALIZING ECONOMIES (NIEs) - The phrase used in the final communique of the 1988 G-7 summit in Toronto to refer to the NICs. The change in terminology was in response to China's objection to references to Taiwan and Hong Kong as "countries." *See Newly Industrializing Countries*

NON-ACTIONABLE SUBSIDY - Government assistance that is permitted under the WTO Agreement on Subsidies and Countervailing Measures, the effective date of which is January 1, 1995. Article 8 of the Agreement defines non-actionable or "green light" subsidies as non-specific (widely available) subsidies; certain assistance for research and development; certain assistance to disadvantaged regions; and certain assistance to promote adaptation to new environmental requirements. Subsidies that do not meet the test for specificity or the limitations and conditions for other non-actionable subsidies are deemed to be actionable and may be subject to countervailing duties or other countervailing measures. *See Actionable Subsidy, Prohibited Subsidy, Specific Subsidy*

NON-DISCRIMINATION - The central principle of the GATT/WTO which prescribes that each country should treat all other countries in the same way with regard to trade. Exceptions to this principle, such as arrangements to benefit less developed countries, or a country's partners in a customs union or a free-trade area, are permitted by the GATT/WTO. *See Most-Favored-Nation Treatment, National Treatment*

NON-GOVERNMENTAL ORGANIZATIONS (NGOs) - In the context of U.S. trade policy, groups such as the Sierra Club, the National Wildlife Federation, Amnesty International, and the AFL-CIO, which, though not government organizations, seek to participate at a working level in making trade policy. In the international context, the term refers to private, not-for-profit groups which seek to shape international programs and the policies of international bodies like the United Nations.

NON-MARKET ECONOMY (NME) - The economic system of a country in which economic activity is regulated by central planning, as opposed to market forces. Production targets, prices, investment allocations, inputs, and most other aspects of economic decision-making are executed in accordance with a national economic plan drawn up by a central planning authority. Such centralized planning is characteristic of the economic systems of communist countries. In U.S. antidumping practice, the "normal value" of an NME product is derived by evaluating each of its factors of production (e.g. labor, raw materials) as they would be in a market economy country of comparable economic development, and then adding amounts for general and administrative expenses, packing, and profit. The United States does not maintain a list of NME's but makes determinations on a case-by-case basis.

NON-PAPER - In trade negotiating terms, a paper circulated for discussion without committing the author's country to the contents.

NON-TARIFF BARRIERS (NTB) - Import quotas, burdensome customs formalities, foreign exchange controls, or other measures or policies (other than tariffs) which restrict or prevent trade.

NON-TARIFF MEASURES (NTM) - A more neutral term than "Non-Tariff Barriers" *(see entry)*, in that it admits of the possibility that measures affecting imports need not be barriers to trade. Such measures might be counting the imported goods, inspecting them, etc.

NORMAL TRADE RELATIONS (NTR) - The U.S. equivalent of most-favored-nation (MFN) treatment *(see entry)*. The Congress approved the change in terminology in mid-1998 on the grounds that all but six countries receive MFN treatment. The six are Afghanistan, Cuba, Laos, North Korea, Vietnam, and Yugoslavia.

NORMAL VALUE - In antidumping practice, this is another term for "fair value" *(see entry)*. In order of preference, normal value is determined on the basis of home-market sales, third-country sales, or constructed value.

NORTH AMERICAN FREE TRADE AGREEMENT (NAFTA) - A free trade agreement that entered into force in January 1994, among Canada, Mexico, and the United States aimed at eliminating nearly all barriers to trade and investment in the region. Tariffs are to be eliminated, and quotas and investment restrictions phased out, within 10 years for most products and sectors, and within 15 years for others. Exceptions to the program of free trade and investments include trade in agricultural products between Canada and the other two partners; cultural industries; and petroleum exploration and production. NAFTA includes enforceable dispute settlement mechanisms. *See U.S.-Canada Free Trade Agreement*

NORTH AMERICAN INDUSTRY CLASSIFICATION SYSTEM (NAICS) - In 1997, the NAICS replaced the Standard Industrial Classification (SIC) *(see entry)* as the official classification system for all businesses and establishments. The NAICS uses a six digit code system allowing it to include newer industries and incorporate categories according to a production/process-oriented basis. The NAICS was jointly created by the U.S. Census Bureau, the U.S. Economic Classification Policy Committee, Statistics Canada, and Mexico's Instituto Nacional de Estatistica, Geografia y Informatica. This system is used widely across Canada, Mexico, and the United States.

NORTH-SOUTH TRADE - Trade between developed market economies (North) and developing countries (South).

NORTHERN TRIANGLE - Guatemala, Honduras, and El Salvador, in the context of their negotiations for a free trade agreement with Mexico.

NOTIFICATION - In the context of the GATT/WTO, the procedure whereby a country taking, or planning to take, a trade-restrictive measure informs the Secretariat, which then passes the information on to the Members.

NULLIFICATION OR IMPAIRMENT - The adverse economic effect on one WTO signatory caused by another WTO party's trade action. Nullification or impairment of WTO rights and obligations may give rise to a formal action under WTO dispute settlement procedures.

O

OFFER LIST - The concessions offered by a country in a trade negotiation, or a list of selected commodities on which a country offers to make concessions. The actual list submitted during the negotiations may include a catalogue of exceptions to an agreed formula for tariff reductions, or an offer to expand the coverage of a proposed code. *See Codes of Conduct, Concessions*

OFFICE OF DEFENSE TRADE CONTROLS (ODTC) - An office in the Bureau of Political-Military Affairs of the U.S. State Department responsible for controlling the export and import of military articles and services. The office handles requests for approval of weapons exports, including some dual-use items, and monitors compliance with U.S. export restrictions on arms.

OFFICE OF FOREIGN ASSETS CONTROLS (OFAC) - An office in the U.S. Treasury Department responsible for enforcing financial and trade sanctions against targeted foreign countries, terrorist organizations, and international narcotics traffickers. The decision to impose sanctions is usually made by the President, on the advice of the National Security Council. Once the decision is made, much of the implementation work is assigned to OFAC.

OFFICE OF TEXTILES, APPAREL AND CONSUMER GOODS (OTEXA) - An office within the U.S. Department of Commerce whose personnel oversee programs and strategies to improve the domestic and international competitiveness of the U.S. fiber, textile, and apparel industries, as well as industries that manufacture a wide range of related consumer products. The Deputy Assistant Secretary

(DAS) of OTEXA serves as chairman of the Committee for the Implementation of Textile Agreements (CITA) *(see entry)*, which determines when market-disrupting factors exist in the domestic fiber, textile, and apparel marketplace.

OFFSET REQUIREMENTS - Obligations imposed by the governments of countries making significant foreign purchases, or permitting significant foreign investments, on the parties providing those things. Governments sometimes impose such obligations in exchange for approval of major purchases of military or high-cost civilian goods, in an effort either to reduce the adverse balance-of-trade impacts of the purchases, or to gain specified industrial benefits. Offset requirements generally take one of two forms: (1) the foreign supplier is required to purchase locally produced goods or services; or (2) the foreign supplier is required to establish manufacturing facilities in the importing country or to purchase there some of the components used in manufacturing the product.

OLIGOPOLY - A market structure in which several firms control prices, but no single one holds a monopolistic position. If price collusion occurs, the association becomes known as a cartel. *See Monopoly, Cartel*

OMNIBUS TRADE AND COMPETITIVENESS ACT OF 1988 - *See Appendix IV*

OPEN DOOR POLICY - A policy that treats citizens and products of a foreign country in the same way as domestic citizens and products. *See Most Favored Nation Treatment*

OPEN SKIES - A U.S. policy to seek bilateral agreements on air transportation, in order to loosen restrictions on market access and prices. The United States first embraced the open skies concept in a 1992 Air Service Agreement with the Netherlands. Subsequently, the United States has concluded open sky agreements with Austria, Belgium, Brunei, Costa Rica, Czech Republic, Denmark, El Salvador, Finland, Germany, Guatemala, Honduras, Iceland, Jordan, Luxembourg,

Nicaragua, Norway, Panama, Singapore, Sweden, Switzerland, and Taiwan.

ORDERLY MARKETING AGREEMENTS (OMAs) - Agreements negotiated between trading partners in which the exporting nation undertakes to ensure that its exports of specified "sensitive" products will not disrupt, threaten, or harm competitive industries or workers in importing countries. In practical terms, this usually entails the establishment of an export licensing system and export quotas for the goods in question. The Uruguay Round Agreement on Safeguards places tight disciplines on the use of OMAs and similar quantitative restrictions. *See Voluntary Restraint Agreements*

ORGANIZATION FOR ECONOMIC COOPERATION AND DEVELOPMENT (OECD) - An organization established in 1960 as a forum for the developed, free market countries to discuss trade and related matters, and as an economic research center. The OECD periodically publishes analyses of member countries' economies, with projections for economic growth. It also provides technical support for discussions, which it hosts, on topics of interest to its member states. In recent years, OECD work on investment and bribery has been particularly noteworthy. The OECD member countries are Australia, Austria, Belgium, Canada, Czech Republic, Denmark, Finland, France, Germany, Greece, Hungary, Iceland, Ireland, Italy, Japan, Luxembourg, Mexico, Netherlands, New Zealand, Norway, Poland, Portugal, South Korea, Spain, Sweden, Switzerland, Turkey, United Kingdom, and United States. In addition, the Commission of the European Union generally takes part in the work of the OECD.

ORGANIZATION OF AFRICAN UNITY (OAU) - Headquartered in Addis Ababa, Ethiopia, this organization was founded in May 1963 by 32 African countries and has since expanded to include 53 members. The OAU strives to promote African unity; balance political, economic, cultural, scientific, and defense policies; and abolish colonialism. The members are Algeria, Angola, Benin, Botswana, Burkina Faso, Burundi, Cameroon, Cape Verde, Central African Republic, Chad, Comoros, Congo (Republic), Congo (Democratic

Republic), Cote d'Ivoire, Djibouti, Egypt, Equatorial Guinea, Eritrea, Ethiopia, Gabon, Gambia, Ghana, Guinea, Guinea-Bissau, Kenya, Lesotho, Liberia, Libya, Madagascar, Malawi, Mali, Mauritania, Mauritius, Mozambique, Namibia, Niger, Nigeria, Rwanda, Sao Tome and Principe, Senegal, Seychelles, Sierra Leone, Somalia, South Africa, Sudan, Swaziland, Tanzania, Togo, Tunisia, Uganda, West Sahara (Sahrawi Arab Democratic Republic), Zambia, and Zimbabwe.

ORGANIZATION OF AMERICAN STATES (OAS) - A regional organization created in Bogota, Colombia in April 1948 (entered into force December 1951) that promotes Latin American economic and social development. Members include Antigua and Barbuda, Argentina, Bahamas, Barbados, Belize, Bolivia, Brazil, Canada, Chile, Colombia, Costa Rica, Cuba (participation suspended), Dominica, Dominican Republic, Ecuador, El Salvador, Grenada, Guatemala, Guyana, Haiti, Honduras, Jamaica, Mexico, Nicaragua, Panama, Paraguay, Peru, St. Kitts and Nevis, St. Lucia, St. Vincent and the Grenadines, Suriname, Trinidad and Tobago, United States, Uruguay, and Venezuela. The U.S. accredits an Ambassador to the OAS. The OAS secretariat is located in Washington, D.C. The forerunner of the OAS was the Pan American Union *(see entry)* which lasted from 1910 until the founding of the OAS.

ORGANIZATION OF EASTERN CARIBBEAN STATES (OECS) - An eight-member sub-group of CARICOM *(see entry)* from the English-speaking Caribbean including Antigua and Barbuda, British Virgin Islands, Dominica, Grenada, Montserrat, St. Kitts and Nevis, St. Lucia, and St. Vincent and the Grenadines. Member countries share a common currency and central bank, in addition to their common language.

ORGANIZATION OF PETROLEUM EXPORTING COUNTRIES (OPEC) - Headquartered in Vienna, this cartel of petroleum exporting countries was formed in 1960 to increase the coordination and unification of the petroleum policies of member countries, and the protection of their individual and collective interests. The members are Algeria, Ecuador, Gabon, Indonesia, Iran, Iraq, Kuwait,

Libya, Nigeria, Qatar, Saudi Arabia, United Arab Emirates, and Venezuela.

OVERSEAS PRIVATE INVESTMENT CORPORATION (OPIC) - The U.S. agency whose purpose is to promote U.S. private investment in developing nations and economies in transition. Its primary activity is providing insurance against political risk.

P

PACIFIC ECONOMIC COOPERATION GROUP - An organization of Pacific Rim nations (and Taiwan): Australia, Brunei, Canada, Chile, China, Colombia, Hong Kong, Indonesia, Japan, Malaysia, Mexico, New Zealand, Peru, Philippines, Russian Federation, Singapore, South Korea, the South Pacific Forum Island Nations, Taiwan, Thailand, and the United States. Vietnam joined in 1994 as an associate member. The organization was established in 1980 to advance economic cooperation and market-driven integration. Syn. *Pacific Economic Cooperation Conference*

PACKAGING, LABELING AND MARKETING REGULATIONS - National requirements that oblige exporters to offer their goods in certain kinds of containers or to identify the contents in particular ways. Even when designed only to protect consumers, such requirements may pose more problems for the makers of imported goods than for domestic producers, and thus may be regarded as non-tariff measures that inhibit trade.

PAN AMERICAN UNION - *See Organization of American States*

PANELS OF EXPERTS - Special committees established by the WTO on an ad hoc basis to study particular facets of WTO work or to examine complaints brought by WTO members against fellow members. Panels are generally composed of three persons who serve in their individual capacities, acting not as representatives of nations but as experts or objective judges of particular matters.

PARALLEL IMPORTS - Goods which are imported into one country by both an intended exclusive distributor and a second party who has obtained the goods from a third party. Also refers to goods which are authorized to be sold in one country, but are sold in another country without the consent of the owner.

PARIS CLUB - A popular designation for meetings between representatives of a developing country that wishes to renegotiate its "official" debt (normally excluding private sector debts without official guarantees) and representatives of the relevant creditor governments and international institutions. These meetings usually occur at the request of a debtor country that wishes to consolidate debt service payments falling due over a specified period. Meetings are traditionally chaired by a senior official of the French Treasury Department. Comparable meetings occasionally take place in London or New York for countries wishing to renegotiate repayment terms for their debts to private banks; those meetings are sometimes called "creditor clubs."

PARIS CONVENTION - An international agreement for the protection of intellectual property, originally concluded among 11 states in 1883. Since that time it has been revised six times and currently has 108 signatories. In this treaty, intellectual property includes patents, utility models, industrial designs, trademarks, trade names, and service marks. The basic provisions of the Paris Convention can be divided into two parts: those which guarantee "national treatment" *(see entry)* in each of the member countries, and those which establish the principle of "right of priority." Right of priority allows a person to enjoy all intellectual property protection rights for a product in any country in which an application has been filed within twelve months of the original filing. *See Intellectual Property Rights*

PART FOUR OF GATT - GATT Articles XXXVI, XXXVII and XXXVIII, which deal with the development needs of the less-developed signatory countries.

PASS-THROUGH - Trading operations that involve a trader's use of one country in a trade bloc as a means of gaining preferential treatment from other countries in the bloc.

PATENT - The exclusive right to manufacture and market a product, granted to its inventor by a government for a legally prescribed time. *See Paris Convention*

PAYMENTS AND TRANSFERS - In the context of international business, profits, dividends, royalties, fees and other contractual payments remitted across borders. Most multilateral trade and investment agreements permit some restrictions on transfers.

PECO (Pays de l'Europe Centrale et Orientale) - The French term used by the European Union to refer to the "countries of Central and Eastern Europe" following the break-up of the Soviet bloc in 1989-90.

PERFORMANCE REQUIREMENTS - *See Export Performance Requirements*

PERIOD OF INVESTIGATION - In U.S. antidumping and countervailing duty practice, normally a six-month period beginning at least 150 days prior to, and continuing 30 days after, the first day of the month in which an AD or CVD petition is filed. During this time, an exporter's home market prices (or prices on sales to third countries), U.S. market prices, and other relevant matters are investigated to determine whether sales to the United States have been at less than fair value. For purposes of injury determinations, the U.S. International Trade Commission normally gathers data on the previous three calendar years.

PHYTOSANITARY REGULATIONS - *See Sanitary and Phytosanitary Regulations*

PIPELINE PROTECTION - Broadly, the provisional protection accorded to inventors by a country prior to the grant of formal patent protection for such inventions. More narrowly, temporary safeguards against the copying of inventions, processes, or new products, usually in the pharmaceutical or agri-chemical fields, accorded by a government to its home-country firms or individuals prior to the granting of formal patent protection.

PLANNED MARKET ECONOMY - One of a number of terms coined by China to describe its economy. It is meant to distinguish China from both market and non-market economies. *Syn. Command Economy*

PLAZA ACCORD - The agreement set out in a communiqué issued by the finance ministers and central bank governors of the G-5 countries (US, Great Britain, France, Germany, and Japan), who met in September 1985 at the Plaza Hotel in New York City to address problems arising from the appreciation of the dollar. The communiqué stated that the ministers favored an appreciation of the other four currencies against the dollar, and central bank intervention to support that goal. *See Louvre Accord*

PLURILATERAL - Having to do with, or involving, a few countries. This differs from "multilateral" which refers to a large number of countries — usually all those interested in a given matter.

PLURILATERAL AGREEMENT - In the context of the World Trade Organization, an international trade agreement which binds only its signatories rather than all WTO members. A plurilateral agreement creates rights and obligations among only signatories to it. Plurilateral agreements are effectively treaties separate from the WTO Agreement even though they were negotiated under the auspices of, and are administered by, the WTO. Annex 4 of the WTO Agreement contains four plurilateral agreements: (1) the Agreement on Trade in Civil Aircraft, (2) the Agreement on Government Procurement, (3) the International Dairy Agreement, and (4) the International Bovine Meat Agreement *(see entries)*.

POLICY FRAMEWORK PAPER (PFP) - A document which recites steps a country will take in consideration of structural adjustment assistance (usually including budgetary support) from the International Monetary Fund. A Policy Framework Paper also describes the origins of the country's difficulties, a diagnosis as to the efforts needed to overcome the country's economic and financial problems, requisite financing, and the probable impacts of the adjustment program on the beneficiary country's environment and society. The paper, updated annually, is developed by the recipient government in collaboration with IMF and the World Bank. By design, it also serves as a vehicle for attracting assistance from other donors. *See Enhanced Structural Adjustment Facility*

POLITICAL RISK - With regard to payment guarantees of the U.S. Eximbank and the U.S. Overseas Private Investment Corporation *(see entry)*, the danger of defaults or losses due to expropriations or other action or inaction by governments; war and civil unrest; and inconvertibility of local currency to dollars. Currency devaluations are not considered political risks. Eximbank and OPIC may extend insurance against trade losses arising from political risks. *See Commercial Risk*

PREDATORY DUMPING - Dumping with the intent and/or effect of injuring or destroying competitors.

PREEMPTION - The right of U.S. Customs to seize and sell products that have been deliberately undervalued by an importer in order to avoid payment of duties, or to reduce the amount paid.

PREFERENCES - Special trading advantages extended by importing countries to selected trading partners. The benefits usually consist of tariff rates below those imposed on goods of other supplier countries, or exemptions of the favored countries from certain non-tariff barriers. *See Generalized System of Preferences, Reverse Preferences*

PRELIMINARY DETERMINATION - In U.S. antidumping and countervailing duty proceedings, an initial determination made by the Department of Commerce or the U.S. International Trade Commission.

Within 45 days of the filing of a petition, the USITC must determine whether there is a "reasonable indication" of material injury or a threat thereof. If affirmative, the investigation continues; if negative, it is terminated immediately. The Commerce Department's preliminary determination normally is made within 140 days after initiation (190 days if extended) in antidumping cases and within 65 days (130 days if extended) in countervailing duty cases. If affirmative, suspension of liquidation *(see entry)* is ordered and bonds or cash deposits are required equal to the estimated margin of dumping or the net countervailable subsidy. If negative, the Commerce investigation proceeds to a final determination without a suspension of liquidation. In Canada, the duty initially collected to offset an estimated amount of dumping or subsidy is called a "provisional duty."

PRICE DISCRIMINATION - The practice of charging different buyers different prices for the same merchandise. Depending on its effects, this practice may be illegal under U.S. antitrust laws and certain international trade agreements.

PRICE ELASTICITY - A measure of the responsiveness of consumers to price changes. For example, if a restaurant raises its prices by 15 percent, what will be the effect on its business? Defined exactly, price elasticity measures the probable percentage change in demand for a given product in response to a one-percent change in its price.

PRICE UNDERTAKING - An agreement to settle an antidumping case by raising the price of an exported good to a level sufficient to eliminate injury to producers of similar goods in the importing country. Seldom used in U.S. practice, price undertakings are common in the EU, Canadian and Australian antidumping regimes.

PRICE-AVERAGING CALCULATIONS - In U.S. antidumping practice, the use of weighted averages in comparing the exporting country's home market prices for goods to the export prices of the same merchandise.

PRIMARY COMMODITIES - Commodities, including agricultural products, in a raw or unprocessed state. For example, iron ore is a primary commodity, whereas pig iron is a semi-processed product, and a steel girder is a manufactured item.

PRIMARY PRODUCTS - *See Primary Commodities*

PRINCIPAL SUPPLIER - The country that has the largest portion of total WTO trade in a given product imported into a given country. The principal supplier to a given country of a given product, and the country holding initial negotiating rights *(see entry)* with regard to that product/country, have the first rights to negotiate compensation should the importing country assess a duty on the product in excess of its bound rate. Any tariff concessions granted in such negotiations are granted automatically to all other countries which enjoy MFN status.

PRIOR DEPOSITS - The deposit in a commercial bank or central bank by an importer of a specified sum of money (usually a percentage of the value of contemplated imports) for a specified length of time. These deposits, when required by the government of the importing country as a condition of importing, are often held without interest and thus represent a barrier to trade.

PRIORITY FOREIGN COUNTRY - A designation under "Special 301" intellectual property provisions of U.S. trade law applied to those foreign countries that provide the least adequate protection of U.S. intellectual property rights and which are not engaged in good faith negotiations or making significant progress in negotiations to address these problems. Once a country has been named to the PFC list by the U.S. Trade Representative, the USTR must decide within 30 days whether to initiate a formal investigation of that country's policies and practices with regard to intellectual property.

PRIORITY WATCH LIST (PWL) - In the context of the "Special 301" provisions of U.S. trade law, a list of countries which do not provide adequate protection of US intellectual property rights or fair market access to US persons who rely on IP protections. Countries on the

PWL are not considered to be as deficient in their handling of intellectual property rights as countries placed on the "Priority Foreign Country" list under the Special 301 clause.

PROCESSING AND PRODUCTION METHODS (PPMs) - The means by which something is made, as distinguished from the materials from which it is made. There is longstanding debate in international trade circles as to the desirability and practicality of trying to afford some measure of protection against the unauthorized copying of PPMs.

PROCLAMATION AUTHORITY - A delegation of authority from the U.S. Congress to the President to negotiate and implement tariff reductions within certain guidelines. Section 101 of the Trade Act of 1974 provided the President with "proclamation" authority for a five-year period to implement tariff reductions negotiated in the Tokyo Round, without having to seek congressional approval. The other Tokyo Round agreements, however, did require affirmative action by the U.S. Congress.

PRODUCER SUBSIDY EQUIVALENT (PSE) - The percentage of a producer's total revenue from the sales of one or more products that is attributable to direct or indirect government transfers. *See Consumer Subsidy Equivalent*

PROFESSIONAL SERVICES - The work product of highly trained specialists in fields like law, accounting, architecture, auditing, engineering, medicine, etc. Professional services are a sizable export industry for the U.S. and an important contributor to the services export surplus. The WTO has established the GATS to develop disciplines on domestic regulations that act as barriers to trade; to encourage the use of international standards; and to develop guidelines for Mutual Recognition Agreements. *See GATS*

PROHIBITED SUBSIDY - Under Article III of the WTO Agreement on Subsidies and Countervailing Measures, members are prohibited from granting subsidies that are contingent on export performance or on the use of domestic products in preference to imported goods. Agricultural goods are exempted from this prohibition. The prohibition applies without regard to trade effects. Prohibited subsidies are referred to as "red light" subsidies. *See Countervailable Subsidy, Non-actionable Subsidy*

PROHIBITIVE DUTY - A tariff rate that is high enough to prevent imports. Usually used to protect infant industry from foreign imports or to retaliate against a country's trade practice.

PROTECTION - In the trade context, government measures, including both tariff and non-tariff measures, that raise the cost of imported goods or otherwise restrict their entry and thus strengthen the competitive position of domestic goods.

PROTECTIONISM - The policy of setting trade barriers high enough to discourage imports, or high enough to raise prices sufficiently to allow relatively inefficient domestic producers to compete successfully with imports. These barriers "protect" domestic producers from lower-priced foreign goods.

PROTOCOL OF ACCESSION - The legal document that recognizes a country's rights and obligations consequent upon signing an international agreement or joining an organization (e.g., the WTO).

PROTOCOL OF PROVISIONAL APPLICATION (PPA) - A legal device that enabled the original contracting parties of the GATT to "grandfather" existing domestic practices that would otherwise be inconsistent with GATT obligations. *See Grandfather Clause*

PROVISIONAL ACCESSION - A theoretically temporary status of membership in the WTO which enables a country to enjoy the benefits of membership for the time needed to phase out those of its policies that are inconsistent with the WTO agreement.

PROVISIONAL DUTY - *See Preliminary Determination*

PUBLIC INTEREST - A provision included in some national antidumping legislation that permits or requires authorities to take into account broader national interests in deciding whether to apply antidumping remedies, and in determining the size of duties. In the European Union, this provision is called "Community interest." The U.S. has no public interest provision in its antidumping or countervailing laws.

PUNTA DEL ESTE DECLARATION - The September, 1986, declaration that launched the Uruguay Round of GATT negotiations. The declaration, approved by the contracting parties and their trade ministers, included a statement of objectives and an agenda for the round.

PURCHASING POWER PARITY (PPP) - In the context of international finance, the evaluation of the relative worth of two currencies by their purchasing power in their home countries. Thus, if the same basket of goods costs 36,000 Belgian Francs in Belgium and 6,000 French Francs in France, the "parity" in terms of purchasing power is 6 BF = 1 FF.

PYRAMID OF PRIVILEGE - A perception, mainly by third world countries, that they are at the bottom of a pyramid that protects certain developed countries' industries from low-cost imports from the third world.

Q

QUADRILATERAL MEETINGS - Informal meetings of the trade ministers of the U.S., the European Union, Canada and Japan, to discuss trade policy matters.

QUALIFICATION REQUIREMENTS - Standards set by national governments or certification bodies to ensure minimum quality of professional services within their domestic markets, and to verify the competence of foreign professionals. Under the WTO Agreement on Technical Barriers to Trade, qualification requirements must not constitute unnecessary barriers to trade in services. Nonetheless, even nondiscriminatory standards may restrict trade if they differ from country to country.

QUALIFIED MAJORITY - The number of votes required for a decision to be adopted in the European Council, currently 62 of 87 votes. Votes are weighted as follows: France, Germany, Italy and the United Kingdom, 10 each; Spain, 8; Belgium, Greece, the Netherlands and Portugal, 5 each; Austria and Sweden, 4 each; Denmark, Ireland and Finland, 3 each; and Luxembourg, 2. The weighting represents a compromise between the equality of member states and their relative populations.

QUANTITATIVE RESTRICTIONS (QRs) - Specific limits on the quantity or value of goods that can be imported or exported during a specific time period. GATT Article XI generally prohibits the use of quantitative restrictions except under specified conditions. The WTO Agreement on Safeguards elaborates on and seeks to strengthen those conditions.

QUINTS - An informal term for the members of a group of agricultural ministers who meet to discuss world agricultural trade issues. The informal group consists of Australia, Canada, the European Union, Japan, and the U.S.

QUOTA AUCTIONING - *See Import Quota Auctioning*

QUOTA - *See Import Quota, Export Quota*

R

RECIPROCITY - The principle governing WTO negotiations under which governments extend comparable concessions to each other. Historically, developing countries have not been obliged to offer fully reciprocal concessions to developed countries. The Uruguay Round attempted to redress this imbalance by integrating into the WTO agreement itself most existing plurilateral codes and the new provisions in such areas as services, thereby obligating all Members somewhat more equally.

RECTIFICATIONS - Changes made to a country's schedule of WTO concessions, usually involving only correction of errors, but occasionally involving limited duty changes or withdrawal of items from a schedule as a result of the negotiated settlement of a dispute.

RED CLAUSE - An authorization in a commercial letter of credit for the advising/negotiating bank to make an advance to the seller before the goods involved are shipped to the buyer. Such advances can be made for up to 100% of the shipment value, but are usually for less. *See Letter of Credit*

RED SUBSIDY - *See Prohibited Subsidy*

REGIONAL SUBSIDY - Preferential support from a government to assist one or more of its geographic regions in promoting economic development or in advancing social objectives. The Mezzogiorno Region of southern Italy has long benefited from regional subsidies. Under the Uruguay Round Agreement on Subsidies and Countervailing Measures,

WTO Members are permitted to provide regional subsidies in specified circumstances.

REGIONAL VALUE CONTENT METHOD - A North American Free Trade Agreement (NAFTA) procedure applicable when specified in the Annex 401 rules of origin. This method is used to determine the origin of goods based on the place where significant value is added through manufacturing or processing. Typically, when added value equals or exceeds a percentage of an article's original value, origin is ascribed to the country in which value was added. For example, if goods made up of components originating in China have 50% added to their overall value by virtue of processing in Mexico, then Mexico is the final product's country of origin. If the Chinese components had not undergone substantial change in Mexico and their overall value had not increased significantly, the country of origin would remain China. Regional value content determinations are often required to asses a product's eligibility for a NAFTA tariff preference. Regional value content rules are commonly applied to products of the automotive and chemical industries.

RELATED PARTY - As defined in Section 771 of the Tariff Act of 1930 *(see entry),* a producer and an exporter or importer are considered related parties if (1) the producer "directly or indirectly controls" the exporter or importer, (2) the exporter or importer "directly or indirectly controls" the producer, (3) a third party "directly or indirectly controls" the producer and the exporter or importer, or (4) the producer and the exporter or the importer "directly or indirectly control" a third party. A party is considered to "directly or indirectly control" another party if the party is "legally or operationally in a position to exercise restraint or direction over the other party." In Canada, the concept of "associated persons" is used to refer to both related parties and others who, while unrelated, do not deal with each other at arm's length.

REQUEST/OFFER PROCEDURE - A negotiating approach wherein requests for trade concessions are submitted by a country to its trading partners, and wherein, as a second step, countries publicize lists of concessions which they are willing to consider. This represents an alternative to the formula-cut tariff approach which has been used in the past two rounds of multilateral trade negotiations.

RESERVATION - A limitation which conditions the acceptance of a trade agreement, usually involving a specific provision that a signatory is unable or unwilling to implement.

RESERVE TRANCHE POSITION - In the context of the International Monetary Fund (IMF), the amount by which the value of an IMF member country's deposit account balance (referred to as the country's "quota") exceeds the value of that country's currency held in the IMF's General Reserve Account, not including any such General Reserve Account holding which resulted from the country's purchase of other currencies with its own currency. A member country facing balance-of-payment difficulties may use its currency to purchase other currencies, up to the full value of the country's reserve tranche position, without charge. A country which draws upon its reserve tranche position in that manner is not deemed to have used IMF credit and is neither obliged nor expected to repurchase its own currency. *See Credit Tranches, International Monetary Fund*

RESTITUTIONS - Certain payments made by the European Union (EU) to exporters of processed agricultural products made from raw materials for which the processor paid higher-than-world prices as a result of EU programs. In theory, the payments do not subsidize the exports, but merely lower their price to the level at which they would have been in the absence of the EU programs.

RESTRAINT OF TRADE - Collusion among two or more competitors who attempt to restrict trade in some manner.

RESTRICTIVE BUSINESS PRACTICES (RBP) - Activities of private firms or public institutions that limit access to markets or otherwise restrain competition.

RETALIATION - Action taken by a country to redress the adverse effects of increased tariffs or other trade restrictions of another country.

The WTO permits such redress if the country taking the initial action fails to make offsetting concessions satisfactory to its trading partner(s). The amount of trade affected by such retaliatory measures should be commensurate with the amount of trade adversely affected by the initial import protection.

REVALUATION - In the context of a system of fixed currency exchange rates, the increase in the relative value of a currency due to actions of the government which issues that currency. *See Devaluation*

REVERSE PREFERENCES - Tariff advantages formerly offered by developing countries to imports from certain developed countries that granted them preferences. Reverse preferences characterized trading arrangements between the European Union and some developing countries, notably the former colonies of EU member states, prior to the advent of the Generalized System of Preferences and the signing of the Lomé Convention. *See European Union, Generalized System of Preferences, Lomé Convention, Preferences*

RIGHT OF ESTABLISHMENT - The right of an investor from one country to make a direct investment in another country for the purpose of establishing a business or other enterprise there.

RIO GROUP - A political forum of Latin American and Caribbean countries that promotes regional political, economic and social cooperation. The group was set up in Rio de Janeiro, Brazil, in 1986. Its membership is the same as ALADI's: Argentina, Bolivia, Brazil, Colombia, Chile, Ecuador, Mexico, Paraguay, Peru, Uruguay and Venezuela; and two rotating members that represent the Central American countries and the Caribbean nations. *See ALADI*

ROAD TAXES - Fees imposed by governments on the sale or operation of motor vehicles, typically based on either weight or engine displacement. Road taxes have sometimes been designed to fall more heavily on imported vehicles than on domestically produced ones.

ROBINSON-PATMAN ACT - The 1936 trade legislation, formally Section 2 of the Clayton Act *(see entry)*, which deals with price discrimination. The law makes it illegal for any firm engaged in interstate or foreign commerce to discriminate in price between different buyers for the same commodity, if the effect of the discrimination is to substantially lessen competition or to create a monopoly.

ROLLBACK - Under the Uruguay Round "rollback" commitment, all participants undertook to phase out or bring into conformity with GATT rules all trade-restrictive or trade-distorting measures inconsistent with the GATT or the various GATT codes. Participants are not to seek reciprocal concessions for "rollback" measures.

ROUND - One of the series of multilateral trade negotiations under the auspices of the GATT/WTO, culminating in trade agreements to reduce tariffs or non-tariff barriers among participating countries. *See Appendix III*

RULES OF ORIGIN - Laws and policies used to differentiate between internationally traded goods originating in one country and those originating in another, for the purpose of applying trade measures such as tariffs.

S

SAFEGUARDS - Temporary restrictions on imports. The WTO Agreement on Safeguards recognizes (1) a country's right to impose temporary import controls to prevent or remedy injury to a domestic industry, and (2) the corresponding right of suppliers to that country not to be deprived arbitrarily of access to its markets. Article XIX of the GATT 1994 permits a country to impose temporary import restrictions on a product that is "being imported in such increased quantities and under such conditions as to cause or threaten serious injury." A country which takes a safeguard action is expected to extend compensatory trade benefits to countries adversely affected by the action; if it does not, affected countries may be authorized to redress the situation by their own actions (commonly referred to as "retaliation"). U.S. safeguard actions are regulated by Section 201 of the Trade Act of 1974 *(see entry)*.

SANCTION - A penalty or coercive measure used by one or more countries against another country to influence the target country's conduct, or to pressure the country to stop violating an international agreement or treaty.

SANITARY AND PHYTOSANITARY REGULATIONS - Government laws, decrees, regulations, requirements and procedures applied to protect human, animal and plant life or health. The measures may apply to animals and plants and their products to help ensure that they are safe for consumption and not damaging to the environment. Phytosanitary regulations apply only to plants and plant products. To prevent sanitary and phytosanitary regulations from serving as non-tariff barriers, the Agreement on the Application of Sanitary and

Phytosanitary Measures *(see entry)* was drawn up in the Uruguay Round.

SCHEDULE OF CONCESSIONS - The list of import duties applicable to specified goods which a GATT/WTO member has agreed to reduce and bind, or bind at published rates.

SCHEDULES OF SPECIFIC COMMITMENTS - Article XX of the WTO General Agreement on Trade in Services (GATS) *(see entry)* stipulates that each Member must provide a schedule of the specific commitments it has agreed to concerning limitations on market access and national treatment that a country may impose on foreign providers of services. Schedules specify the terms of market access and national treatment, any undertakings relating to additional commitments, the time-frame for implementing any commitments, and the date of entry into force of the commitments. Commitments may be either "specific" to a sector, or "horizontal" if they cover all sectors. Countries may also make an "unbound" commitment in a sector, reserving the right to introduce a new restrictive measure in that sector at a later date.

SCHENGEN AGREEMENT - Named for the small Luxembourg town in which it was negotiated, this agreement was signed on June 14, 1995 by Belgium, France, Germany, Luxembourg, and the Netherlands. The agreement allows for the gradual removal of common border controls, enhancing freedom of movement for nationals of the signatory states, other EU Member States, and other specified countries. This agreement marks an important step towards the eradication of the European Union's internal borders, but is not a part of the Treaty on European Union.

SCREWDRIVER OPERATION - An assembly plant used to complete a product from imported components. Concern over possible circumvention of antidumping orders by such operations led to a change in U.S. legislation in 1994. *See Anticircumvention*

SECTION 22 - *See Appendix IV*

SECTION 201 - *See Appendix IV, Escape Clause, Safeguards.*

SECTION 232 - *See Appendix IV*

SECTION 301 - *See Appendix IV, Special 301, Super 301*

SECTION 302 - *See Appendix IV*

SECTION 332 - *See Appendix IV*

SECTION 337 - *See Appendix IV*

SECTION 406 - *See Appendix IV*

SECTION 592- *See Appendix IV*

SECTION 751 - *See Appendix IV*

SECTOR-SPECIFIC - Pertaining to a particular economic sector. While the negotiation of trading rules normally takes place without regard to individual product sectors, unusual circumstances have given rise to "sector-specific" negotiations for the aircraft industry, textiles, and a few other product categories.

SECURITY OF INFORMATION SYSTEMS (SIS) - The protection of the availability, integrity and confidentiality of information systems. In 1992 the OECD adopted Guidelines for the Security of Information Systems, the culmination of almost two years' work by the Information, Computer and Communications Policy (ICCP) Committee's carefully chosen "Expert Group." The Expert Group was composed of governmental delegates; scholars in the fields of law, mathematics and computer science; and representatives of the private sector. The term "information systems" includes computers and communication facilities and networks, as well as the information that they process.

SELECTIVITY - The practice of taking trade-restrictive actions against a certain country or a select group of countries as opposed to taking actions on a non-discriminatory (MFN) basis affecting all countries. The WTO Agreement on Safeguards is designed to eliminate selective safeguards.

SEMICONDUCTOR AGREEMENT - A 1986 agreement between the United States and Japan to open the Japanese market to U.S. computer chips and to deter the dumping of Japanese semiconductors in the U.S.. The agreement was set to expire in 1996, but new negotiations in that year brought about an extension until the year 2000.

SENSITIVE PRODUCTS - Goods whose costs of production in a country are so high that any reduction in tariff or non-tariff barriers to imports may threaten the continued viability of domestic producers. Since any significant decline in the competitive situation of such industries may cause social, economic and political problems, "sensitive" products are often exempted from tariff-reduction formulas in trade negotiations. Examples include textiles and steel.

SERIOUS INJURY - *See Injury Determination*

SERVICES - Industries that perform business functions, ancillary to production or distribution, that are usually consumed as they are produced. Examples include advertising, banking, consulting, insurance, telecommunications, tourism and transportation.

736 REVIEW - Section 736 of the U.S. Tariff Act of 1930, as amended, provides for immediate reviews of antidumping orders at the discretion of the Department of Commerce to allow for the posting of a bond or other security as a substitute for the deposit of estimated antidumping duties. An exporter may request that temporary bonds be posted in lieu of cash deposits for up to 90 days after publication of an order to permit calculation of a new dumping margin based on imports occurring after the imposition of the provisional duty. The statute requires that such import transactions be in normal commercial quantities and in the "normal course of trade."

SHADOW ECONOMY - An informal economy that is similar to a black market.

SHERMAN ACT - The first U.S. anti-monopoly law, enacted in 1890. Section 1 outlines a general antitrust prohibition against contracts, combinations, and conspiracies which will restrict either foreign or domestic U.S. trade. Section 2 prohibits forming or conspiring to form a monopoly within the United States or abroad. Violations of this act can be either criminal or civil in nature. Criminal offenses are punishable by fines of up to ten million dollars or imprisonment for up to three years. Civil offenses may be punishable by injunctive or treble damage relief. The language of the Sherman Act was simple, general, and limited in scope, leaving the courts to determine its application. Enactment of the Sherman Act was followed by passage of the Clayton Act *(see entry)* and the Webb-Pomerene Act *(see entry)* to further define U.S. anti-competition laws.

SHERPA - The subcabinet official in each of the large industrial democracies who prepares for her or his government's participation in the annual economic summit meetings. The term is taken from the name given to guides who escort mountain climbers in the Himalayas.

SHIFT - *See Swing*

SHIPPER'S EXPORT DECLARATION - A document required by U.S. Customs to permit the compilation of data for export statistics, and to enforce control regulations.

SHORT SUPPLY – A shortage of a product. There is a procedure within U.S. trade law whereby a downstream user of a product which is subject to antidumping or countervailing duties may petition the U.S. Government for authority to import a specified amount of such product (absent the duties) needed to meet a documented demand, when he/

she can show that the product is not available from a domestic supplier within the time frame required.

SINGAPORE MINISTERIAL - The first meeting of ministers of WTO Members after entry into force of the WTO, held in Singapore in December, 1996. The main tasks were to review progress in the implementation of the Uruguay Round results and to establish a work program for the WTO. Ministers at Singapore endorsed an agreement to remove duties on information technology products by the year 2000. *See International Technology Agreement*

SINGLE EUROPEAN ACT - A treaty ratified in 1987 primarily to consolidate the earlier, separate treaties establishing the European Coal and Steel Community, the European Economic Community, and the European Atomic Energy Community. The Single European Act treaty included steps towards economic and monetary union, and cooperation in the sphere of foreign policy. This act also replaced unanimous voting within the Council by qualified majority voting in these four fields: the creation of an internal market by 1992; technological research and development; economic and social integration; and the improvement of labor standards. This new voting standard has made for a more efficient and streamlined EC decision-making process.

SINGLE UNDERTAKING - A phrase used to characterize the results of the GATT 1994, notably the establishment of the World Trade Organization *(see entry)*. WTO membership involves adherence to all the agreements, except the four plurilateral agreements. In contrast to the GATT, WTO members may not adhere to selected agreements only. Developed and developing countries are subject to the same disciplines (except for plurilateral agreements, and for certain agreements which allowed the staging of implementation).

SINGLE-COLUMN TARIFF SCHEDULE - A tariff schedule listing only one duty rate for each imported commodity.

SLIPPERY SLOPE - The allegorical place of danger due to trade barriers. The term is often used by anti-protectionists when they argue that one restrictive measure begets another.

SMOOT-HAWLEY ACT - *See Tariff Act of 1930, Appendix IV*

SNAP-BACK PROVISIONS - Provisions in an agreement which allow a signatory to withdraw concessions under specific circumstances, such as a balance of payments deficit.

SOCIAL CHARTER - The concept, popular in Europe, of an unwritten code of fundamental social rights of a nation's citizens, particularly its workers. "Charters" are said to guarantee minimum pay, rights, and conditions for certain workers.

SOCIAL DUMPING - The shift of jobs from developed countries to ones with lower wages and weak labor rules, to take advantage of the lower wages and less stringent regulations and standards.

SOFTWOOD LUMBER AGREEMENT - An agreement between the United States and Canada concerning subsidies given to the Canadian lumber industry. The agreement led to the resolution of a series of contentious U.S. countervailing duty cases against imports of Canadian lumber. Specifically, Canada promised to reduce the amount of softwood lumber exports to the United States, provided the U.S. agreed to refrain from taking any trade action in this area. This agreement will remain in force for five years from the date of its inception, April 1, 1996.

SOGO SOSHA - A multi-faceted Japanese commercial enterprise which handles a comprehensive assortment of merchandise. The underlying purpose of a sogo sosha is to provide a full range of services including distribution, finance and information to facilitate trade flows, and to provide an impetus for continued development of both domestic and international commerce and investment. Mitsubishi is a sogo sosha.

SOUND SCIENCE - As used in discussions about the effects of international trade on the environment, this undefined term refers to the honest use of scientific principles and data. Article II of the WTO

Agreement on the Application of Sanitary and Phytosanitary Measures allows Members to apply necessary sanitary or phytosanitary measures to preserve "human, animal, or plant life." These measures must be based on "scientific principles" and "not maintained without sufficient scientific evidence."

SOUTHERN AFRICA DEVELOPMENT COMMUNITY (SADC) - Led by South Africa, a group of 12 Southern African countries organized to promote trade and development in the area. Other member countries are Angola, Botswana, Lesotho, Malawi, Mozambique, Mauritius, Namibia, Swaziland, Tanzania, Zambia and Zimbabwe.

SOUTH ASIAN ASSOCIATION FOR REGIONAL COOPERATION (SAARC) - A regional cooperative grouping of Bangladesh, Bhutan, India, Maldives, Nepal, Pakistan and Sri Lanka founded in December 1985 to promote the welfare and economic growth of its members. The association is composed of a Council of Ministers, a Standing Committee, several Technical Committees, and a Secretariat which is in turn composed of a Secretary-General, seven Directors, and the General Services staff.

SOUTH-SOUTH TRADE - A term used to refer to trade among the developing nations.

SOUTHERN CONE - The countries of Argentina, Chile, Paraguay, and Uruguay, so named because together their shape represents a cone.

SOVEREIGN COMPULSION - A U.S. legal doctrine wherein anti-trust liability may be avoided when concerted action by private companies is taken at the direction of a government, with penalties for non-compliance. Example: compliance with price undertakings *(see entry)*.

SOVEREIGN IMMUNITY - A government's immunity from suit in its own courts. U.S. legislation contains numerous waivers of this immunity.

SPECIAL 301 - *See Appendix IV*

SPECIAL AND DIFFERENTIAL TREATMENT (S&D) - Preferential treatment for the trade of less developed countries. Article 27 of the WTO Agreement on Subsidies and Countervailing Measures *(see entry)* seeks to accord particular benefits to the exports of developing countries, consistent with their trade, financial and development needs. Although largely eroded by the Uruguay Round's concept of a single undertaking, a certain number of special and differential measures continue, most notably the Generalized System of Preferences (GSP) *(see entry)*. Other proposals for special or differential treatment are the expansion of the product and country coverage of the GSP; the acceleration, for LDC exports, of tariff cuts agreed to in the Tokyo Round; the reduction or elimination of tariff escalation *(see entry)*; special provisions for developing country exports in any new codes of conduct covering non-tariff measures; assurance that any new multilateral safeguard system will contain special provisions for developing country exports; and general acceptance of the principle that developed countries should expect less than full reciprocity for trade concessions they grant to developing countries. *See Reciprocity, Single Undertaking*

SPECIAL DRAWING RIGHTS (SDRs) - An artificial "currency" which serves as a medium of exchange in transactions of the International Monetary Fund (IMF). SDRs were created in 1969 by the IMF for the purpose of establishing a supplemental (to gold) international monetary reserve asset. The unit value of an SDR reflects the exchange value of a basket of currencies of major trading countries.

SPECIAL IMPORT MEASURES ACT (SIMA) - Canadian legislation outlining antidumping and countervailing duty proceedings. SIMA is administered by the Canadian International Trade Tribunal (CITT) *(see entry)* and the Deputy Minister of National Revenue. This law came into force December 1, 1984 and has since been amended to incorporate NAFTA *(see entry)* obligations and to comply with pertinent agreements ensuing from the Uruguay Round *(see entry)*.

SPECIFIC SUBSIDY - A subsidy available to certain beneficiaries only. Under Article II of the WTO Agreement on Subsidies and Countervailing Measures, subsidies other than prohibited subsidies are actionable or countervailable only when they are specific. *See Actionable Subsidy, Countervailable Subsidy, Non-Actionable Subsidy*

SPECIFIC TARIFF - A tariff levied on the basis of some physical unit (pound, bushel, or yard) or count (dozen, thousand). *See Ad Valorem Tariff*

STABEX - A program of the European Union (EU) under the 1975 Lomé Convention designed to stabilize the export earnings which beneficiary developing countries (principally ex-colonies of EU member states) derive from the sale of specified raw materials. Under the STABEX system, the EU and its Lomé partners establish per-unit target prices for commodities (say, $1 per pound of cocoa) prior to the start of the marketing year. At the end of that year, the EU pays to the governments of the exporting countries any shortfall. (In this example, if an exporting country sold 10 million pounds of cocoa at an average price of 90 cents per pound, the STABEX fund would pay the exporting country's government $1 million.) STABEX does not interfere with market prices.

STANDARD INDUSTRIAL CLASSIFICATION SYSTEM (SIC) - A now outmoded system of numbered codes which classified all businesses and establishments according to the products and services they provided. The SIC was created to ease the aggregation, tabulation, and analysis of commercial data and to advance approximation in statistical analysis. The SIC codes were used heavily by business directories, directory databases, and particular federal government data series (i.e. Census of Manufactures, the Census of Real Trade). The SIC was replaced by the North American Industry Classification System (NAICS) *(see entry)* in 1997.

STANDARDS CODE - *See Agreement on Technical Barriers to Trade*

STAND-BY ARRANGEMENT - In the context of international finance, an agreement assuring a member country of the International Monetary Fund (IMF) that it will be able to obtain credit up to a specified limit from the IMF during a given period, as long as the member has met the performance criteria and other terms specified in the arrangement. Stand-by arrangements may be extended up to three years. *See International Monetary Fund*

STANDING - The degree of interest in a matter sufficient to confer eligibility to take legal action concerning it. In U.S. antidumping and countervailing duty proceedings, a petition must be filed by or on behalf of a domestic industry. A petitioner or group of petitioners has standing to file if domestic producers or workers supporting the petition (1) account for at least 25 percent of the total production of the like product and (2) represent more of the total production than the portion of industry which expresses opposition to the petition.

STANDSTILL - A commitment by countries involved in the Uruguay Round of trade negotiations (1) not to take any trade-restrictive or trade-distorting measures inconsistent with the GATT or its various codes; (2) not to take any trade-restrictive or trade-distorting measures beyond those consistent with the legitimate exercise of GATT rights (e.g., safeguard or anti-dumping actions); and (3) not to take trade measures in order to improve negotiating positions.

STATE-TRADING ENTERPRISES (STEs) - Entities (often monopolies) established by governments to import, export and/or produce certain products. Under GATT Article XVI, contracting parties which have state-trading entities are required to operate them on the basis of commercial considerations.

STOCKHOLM TREATY - *See European Free Trade Association*

STRUCTURAL CHANGE - Alterations over time of the relative significance of the productive components of national or international economies. Structural changes can involve shifts in the economic importance of various industries, shifts between regions of large national economies, changes in the composition of exports and imports, and product substitution because of changes in consumer preference or technology. The expansion of an entire economy, or temporary shifts in the relationship of its components as a result of cyclical developments, would not be considered structural changes; however, the evolution of an economy from labor-intensive to capital-intensive production would be a structural change. *See Comparative Advantage*

SUBSIDIES CODE - *See Agreement on Subsidies and Countervailing Measures*

SUBSIDY - An economic benefit granted by a government to individuals or firms. The benefit may be in the form of a direct transfer of funds (e.g. a grant), the forgoing of government revenue (e.g. a tax credit) or the provision of goods and services (e.g. cut-rate electricity). There are two general types of subsidies, export and domestic. An export subsidy is a benefit contingent on exports; a domestic subsidy is a benefit not linked to exports. *See Actionable Subsidy, Export Subsidy, Non-Actionable Subsidy, Prohibited Subsidy, Specific Subsidy*

SUMMARY INVESTIGATION - In U.S. antidumping and countervailing duty practice, a 20-day investigation conducted by the U.S. Commerce Department's International Trade Administration immediately following the filing of an antidumping petition. The investigation is designed to ascertain whether the petition contains sufficient information with respect to sales at "less than fair value" or subsidies, and with respect to any injury or threat of injury to a domestic industry, to warrant the initiation of an antidumping or countervailing duty investigation. Normally, the information submitted is deemed sufficient; it is extremely rare for cases to be terminated at this stage. *See Tariff Act of 1930*

SUNSET REVIEW - In antidumping practice, a review conducted every five years to determine whether revocation ("expiry" in WTO/ GATT terms) of the duty would be "likely to lead to continuation or recurrences of dumping and injury." Similar reviews of countervailing duty orders are conducted regarding the continuation or recurrence of subsidies and injury. In the U.S., sunset reviews are formally called five-year reviews.

SUPER 301 - *See Appendix IV*

SUPPLY ACCESS - The availability to importing countries, at reasonable prices, of raw materials and other essential goods available in producer countries.

SURVEILLANCE - In the context of international trade, the monitoring of countries' trade actions to help ensure that governments honor their obligations under trade agreements.

SUSPENSION AGREEMENT - In U.S. antidumping and countervailing duty proceedings, a means of avoiding the issuance of an order. The Department of Commerce may negotiate an agreement to eliminate the dumping or subsidization, or to eliminate completely the injurious effects of such practices, or to cease exports within six months. Countervailing duty cases and antidumping cases involving non-market economy countries may be suspended on the basis of quantitative restraints on exports. An investigation may be suspended at any time after a preliminary, and before a final, determination is made. No agreement to suspend an investigation may be made unless effective monitoring of the agreement is practicable, and the agreement is determined to be in the public interest.

In Canada, suspension agreements are referred to as "undertakings," and may be submitted to the Canadian Deputy Minister at any time following the preliminary determination and prior to the final determination. During this same time period, foreign governments may also submit undertakings to reduce or eliminate subsidies or to limit the number of subsidized goods exported to Canada.

SUSPENSION OF LIQUIDATION - In the context of U.S. antidumping and countervailing duty proceedings, the withholding, by the U.S. Customs Service, of a definitive determination of the duty owed on an import transaction, pending the outcome of an antidumping or countervailing duty proceeding. Under a suspension of liquidation, U.S. Customs requires each importer of the goods in question to post a cash deposit or bond equal to an estimated amount of the dumping margin *(see entry)* or countervailable subsidy *(see entry)*. After an administrative review (typically years after the entry), U.S. Customs assesses final duties, and collects any additional duties due, or refunds any excess duties that were collected.

SWING - As used in textile agreements, the shift of allowable imports from an under-filled quota to a filled one. Swing provisions usually permit shifts of about five or ten percent of the unfilled quota; thus a swing provision might allow a country to ship 11,000 denim jackets and 9,000 denim jeans instead of 10,000 each as previously agreed. Swing provisions are important to textile exporters because they allow for maximum shipments in the face of unforeseen circumstances. *See Shift*

SWITCH TRADING - A complicated form of barter involving a chain of buyers and sellers in different markets. *See Offsets, Countertrade*

T

TARIFF - A tax on imports. Tariffs may be "specific," i.e., in a fixed amount (five cents per pound, $1 per head); "ad valorem," i.e., a percentage of the value of the product (4% of the price at importation), or "mixed," i.e., a combination of specific and ad valorem (15 cents per item plus 10% of price at importation).

TARIFF - Outside the narrow trade context, a term which means the charge payable for transportation. The term is widely used in this sense with regard to shipments by sea.

TARIFF ACT OF 1930 - *See Appendix IV*

TARIFF ANOMALY - A tariff on raw materials or semi-manufactured goods which is higher than the tariff on the finished product made from them. *See Tariff Escalation*

TARIFF BINDING - The formal commitment to maintain the duty rates on specified goods at or below negotiated levels. Bindings are made pursuant to Article II of GATT 1994. *See Binding, Bound Rates*

TARIFF ESCALATION - The imposition of higher rates of duty on processed goods than on the raw materials from which they are made, and the similarly disproportionate treatment given to more highly processed goods. For instance, the import duty is higher in most countries for petrochemicals than for the petroleum and other raw materials necessary for their production. Countries which export raw materials and semi-processed goods contend that tariff escalation in the countries which buy from them hinders the development of manufacturing industries in the exporting countries.

TARIFF HARMONIZATION - *See Harmonization of Tariffs*

TARIFF PEAK - A customs duty in a country's tariff schedule which is noticeably higher than most other rates in that country's schedule. The reduction of tariff peaks is a frequent objective of trade negotiations.

TARIFF PREFERENCE LEVEL (TPL) - The first tier of a two-tiered tariff system wherein a certain quantity of goods pay one rate while goods exceeding that amount are taxed at a higher rate. Example: goods dutied at 10% of the import price for the first 10,000 units, and 25% for all additional units, in each calendar year have a tariff preference level of 10 percent.

TARIFF RATE QUOTA - *See Tariff Preference Level*

TARIFF REDUCTION - The lowering of one or more customs duties, usually in the context of trade negotiations.

TARIFF SCHEDULE - A comprehensive listing of imported goods, and the import duties applicable to each, which a country's customs officials use to determine how much duty is owed at the time goods are imported.

TARIFF SCHEDULES OF THE UNITED STATES (TSUS) - The U.S. Government listing formerly used to describe and classify imported goods and the duty rates applicable to them. In 1988, it was replaced by the Harmonized Tariff Schedule. *See Harmonized System*

TARIFF SURCHARGE - An import tax, usually assessed at a flat rate, in addition to normal duties. Tariff surcharges are typically short-term, emergency measures taken for balance-of-payments reasons.

TECHNICAL BARRIERS TO TRADE - The requirements of governments that products conform to specified standards of quality, performance, safety or dimensions in order to be imported; or that the products undergo specified tests or certification procedures. The GATT/WTO Agreement on Technical Barriers to Trade provides guidelines in this area, with a view to limiting the adverse trade effects of product standards, certification procedures, and tests. *See Agreement on Technical Barriers to Trade*

TECHNOLOGICAL DUALISM - The situation in which certain industries within a country use modern technology while other industries in the same country use older methods of production.

TECHNOLOGY TRANSFER - The movement of technical knowledge from the place where it was generated and developed, to another place. Technology may be transferred in many ways: by free dissemination (technical journals, conferences, emigration of technical experts, technical assistance programs); by sale (patents); by licensing; or by industrial espionage.

TEMPORARY IMPORTATION UNDER BOND (TIB) - A procedure under Chapter 98, Subchapter XIII, Harmonized Tariff Schedule of the U.S., by which an importer can secure a duty exemption for goods not intended for sale, but for demonstration, testing or repair. The bond is normally twice the amount of the usual import duties and associated payments, and will be available for refund from the Customs Office only if the importer agrees to export the goods within one year from their date of importation.

TERMS OF TRADE - The ratio of the prices of a country's exports to the costs of its imports.

TEXTILE MONITORING BODY (TMB) - A WTO advisory body made up of representatives of major textile importing and exporting countries. The TMB monitors the implementation of the Agreement on Textiles and Clothing and advises on disputes between Members. The United States and the EU hold permanent seats. *See Textile Surveillance Body*

TEXTILE SURVEILLANCE BODY (TSB) - The GATT advisory body which monitored the implementation of the Multifibre Agreement *(see entry)* and handled cases of disputes. The MFA and TSB were terminated on December 31, 1994. The TSB was replaced by the Textile Monitoring Body (TMB) *(see entry).*

TEXTILE VISA - A stamped endorsement on an invoice or on an export control license covering textile exports, executed by the government of the exporter. Textile visas are used to control the export of textile and apparel products to the United States and to prevent unauthorized entry of textile products into the country. *See Export License, Visa System*

TEXTILES - A term which, in the context of international trade, usually encompasses yarn and cloth, and items made from them. There is a special WTO regime for trade in textiles, monitored by a special WTO body, the Textile Monitoring Board *(see entry). See Agreement on Textiles and Clothing*

THIRD COUNTRY DUMPING PROVISION- An amendment to U.S. antidumping laws, added as part of the Uruguay Round Agreements Act. The provision allows the government of a WTO Member to file with the U.S. Trade Representative (USTR) a petition requesting that an investigation be conducted to determine if imports from a third country are being sold in the United States at less than fair value, and alleging that an industry in the petitioning country is materially injured by reason of those imports.

THIRD WORLD - Underdeveloped countries, taken as a group. *See Less Developed Countries*

THIRD WORLD NETWORK (TWN) - An independent non-profit international network of organizations and individuals involved in issues relating to development in the Third World. It conducts research on economic, social and environmental issues pertaining to the South; publishes books and magazines on those topics; organizes and participate in seminars; and provides a platform for southern interests and perspectives in international fora such as UN conferences. The TWN's international secretariat is based in Penang, Malaysia. It has offices in Accra, Geneva, London, Montevideo, and New Delhi. Third World Network has affiliated organizations in several Third World countries, including Bangladesh, Brazil, Ethiopia, Ghana, India, Malaysia, Mexico, Peru, the Philippines, Senegal, South Africa, Thailand, and Uruguay.

THREAT OF INJURY – A determination by the U.S. International Trade Commission in the context of an antidumping or countervailing duty investigation that a domestic industry is threatened with material injury by reason of dumped or subsidized imports. *See Injury Determination*

THRESHOLD VALUE - The dividing line, in terms of the value of a purchase, between transactions which are covered by the WTO Agreement on Government Procurement *(see entry)* and those not covered.

TOKYO ROUND OF TRADE NEGOTIATIONS - The seventh round of GATT trade negotiations, formally initiated by the 1973 Tokyo Declaration and concluded in 1979. The Tokyo Round involved 99 countries, including many developing countries and several Eastern European countries. In addition to cutting tariffs, participants in the Tokyo Round made particular efforts to eliminate, reduce, or discipline non-tariff restrictions of trade, especially with respect to impediments to international trade in agricultural goods. *See Non-Tariff Barriers, Tariff, Appendix III*

TRADE ACT OF 1974 - *See Appendix IV*

TRADE AGREEMENTS ACT OF 1979 - *See Appendix IV*

TRADE AND TARIFF ACT OF 1984 - *See Appendix IV*

TRADE EXPANSION ACT OF 1962 - *See Appendix IV*

TRADE-BALANCING REQUIREMENTS - Measures which condition a firm's permissible imports on a specified level of its exports.

TRADE BARRIERS REGULATION (TBR) - A European Union regulation, adopted in January 1995, aimed at the elimination of trade barriers. The procedures outlined in the TBR allow for industries or enterprises to submit formal complaints to the EU regarding trade barriers. The TBR identifies two distinct types of trade barriers: those which have a negative impact on a European Community market or those which have a negative impact on a third country market. To show that a foreign trade barrier has a negative impact on an EU market, an EU industry must be able to prove financial losses or reduced profits, declining sales, or shrinking market shares. With regard to effects in third markets, a complaint may be submitted by either an enterprise or an industry alleging "adverse trade effects" due to trade barriers. If a complaint is found to be valid, the EU Commission will proceed according to the appropriate dispute settlement procedure, usually the WTO dispute mechanism.

TRADE CREATION - The expansion of trade due to shifts in policy. *See Trade Diversion*

TRADE DEVELOPMENT AGENCY (TDA) - A U.S. Government body, created in 1981, to assist in the creation of jobs for Americans by helping U.S. companies pursue overseas business opportunities. Through the funding of feasibility studies, orientation visits, specialized training grants, business workshops, and various forms of technical assistance, the TDA enables U.S. firms to compete for infrastructure and industrial projects in middle-income and developing countries.

TRADE DIVERSION - A shift in the source of imports due to changes in a country's import policies or practices. For example, the establishment of a customs union will induce countries participating in the new economic unit to import from other countries in the union at least some goods which were previously imported from outside the union. According to some trade theorists, the customs union will raise welfare by allocating resources more efficiently given the condition that the "trade creation" (*see entry*) resulting from the customs union -- new trade that would not have taken place in the absence of the customs union -- exceeds the trade diversion.

TRADE AND ENVIRONMENT POLICY ADVISORY COMMITTEE [USTR] (TEPAC) - A group of 35 private-sector experts, established in 1994, to provide policy advice to the U.S. Trade Representative on issues involving trade and the environment.

TRADE NEGOTIATIONS - *See Round*

TRADE POLICY COMMITTEE (TPC) - The Cabinet-level body within the executive branch of the U.S. Government which determines the trade policy of the Administration. Although established by law, the TPC has been largely supplanted by the National Economic Council *(see entry)*.

TRADE POLICY REVIEW GROUP (TPRG) - The Executive Branch's policy-making body in the trade area. Normally chaired by a Deputy U.S. Trade Representative, the TPRG meets at the level of Under Secretary or Assistant Secretary; issues it fails to resolve are referred to the National Economic Council (*see entry*).

TRADE POLICY REVIEW MECHANISM (TPRM) - A GATT/WTO procedure established in 1988 as a result of negotiations on the functioning of the GATT/WTO system. The TPRM conducts regular evaluations of the trade policies and practices of all WTO Members. The intent of the mechanism is to improve adherence to WTO rules, disciplines and commitments by greater transparency and understanding of contracting parties' trade policies. The trade policies of the four largest trading entities will be subject to review every two years, the 16 next largest every 4 years, and the others every six years, with the possible exception of the least developed nations, which may be reviewed less frequently.

TRADE POLICY STAFF COMMITTEE (TPSC) - The working level interagency committee of the U.S. Government responsible for trade issues. Most TPSC work is done by subcommittees formed to address individual problems. The TPSC is chaired by a senior official of the Office of the United States Trade Representative.

TRADEMARK - A name, symbol, design, device, word, or any combination thereof, used by a merchant or manufacturer to identify his/her goods and distinguish them from those made or sold by others. *See Intellectual Property Rights*

TRADE-RELATED ASPECTS OF INTELLECTUAL PROPERTY PROTECTION (TRIPs) - The WTO Agreement, implemented on January 1, 1995, which deals with intellectual property. The objectives of TRIPs is to promote effective and adequate protection of intellectual property rights and to ensure that such protection is not implemented in ways that obstruct trade. The areas covered by the Agreement are copyrights, trademarks, geographical indicators, industrial designs, patents, and layout designs of integrated circuits.

TRADE-RELATED INVESTMENT MEASURES (TRIMs) - The conditions relating to trade which a country places on its grant of permission for an investment from another country. Typical TRIMs which distort trade are the requirement that only domestic supplies of a material be used; that domestic labor be used; and that a specified amount or percentage of production be exported (export performance requirements). The WTO Agreement on Trade-Related Investment Measures is designed to promote national treatment *(see entry)* in this area.

TRADE-WEIGHTED BASIS - A measurement of average tariffs computed by weighing each tariff rate by the value of imports at that rate, relative to the total value of imports. Tariffs on individual commodities in the Uruguay Round Agreement were reduced on a trade-weighted basis by 33%. Individual commodity tariffs were not uniformly affected, however — many were reduced to zero, while others were left unchanged.

TRANSACTION VALUE - The price paid or payable for merchandise sold for export to the U.S., plus amounts for certain items not included in the price, such as packing costs incurred by the buyer. Transaction value is the preferred basis for customs valuation under the WTO Agreement on Implementation of Article VII of the GATT 1994 *(see Customs Valuation Agreement).*

TRANSATLANTIC BUSINESS DIALOGUE (TABD) - Originally conceived by the late U.S. Secretary of Commerce Ron Brown, the TABD is a forum of European and U.S. business leaders who make concrete recommendations to the European Commission and the U.S. Government on ways to reduce non-tariff barriers to transatlantic trade. The TABD comprises 16 working groups, each led by a European and a U.S. CEO. The working groups include an important one on standards that has played a role in the negotiation of Mutual Recognition Agreements in several sectors. The TABD was launched in November 1995 in Seville, Spain. It has no Secretariat.

TRANSATLANTIC ECONOMIC PARTNERSHIP (TEP) - An initiative launched at the EU-U.S. Summit in London on May 18, 1998, outlining an agreement between the U.S. and the European Union to reinforce and expand their commitment to multilateral and bilateral cooperation and common actions in the fields of trade and investment, through international organizations. Replacing EU Commissioner for External Relations Sir Leon Brittan's proposal for a "New Transatlantic Marketplace," the TEP also builds on the New Transatlantic Agenda, signed in Madrid in 1995. Designed to achieve greater market access for goods, services, and agricultural products, this initiative will focus on improving regulatory procedures regarding standards, testing, and certification; maintaining duty-free conditions for electronic commerce; and reducing red tape in an effort to lower consumer costs.

TRANSIT ZONE - A port of entry in a coastal country that is established as a storage and distribution center for the convenience of a neighboring country lacking adequate port facilities or access to the sea. A transit zone is administered so that goods in transit to and from the neighboring country are not subject to the customs duties, import controls, or many of the entry and exit formalities of the host country. A transit zone is a more limited facility than a foreign trade zone or a free port. For comparison, see *Free Port* and *Foreign Trade Zone.*

TRANSPARENCY - The public nature of trade agreements and practices. In the GATT/WTO system, transparency is an important means to ensure fairness in international trade.

TRANS-TASMAN MUTUAL RECOGNITION ARRANGEMENT- *See ANZCERTA*

TREATY OF PARIS - In the context of European integration, the treaty of April 19, 1951, which established the European Coal and Steel Community (ECSC) *(see entry)*. The treaty will expire in 2002.

TREATY OF ROME - *See European Communities*

TREATY OF STOCKHOLM - *See European Free Trade Association*

TRIBUNAL - *See Canadian International Trade Tribunal (CITT)*

TRIGGER PRICE MECHANISM (TPM) - The system used by the United States from 1978 to 1982 to monitor the price of steel imports in order to detect and deter injurious unfair trade practices in the steel sector. Indicative "trigger" prices were determined according to the estimated landed costs of the world's most efficient producer (for most of this period, Japan) for imported steel. If a foreign producer sold steel in the United States below the "trigger," formal anti-dumping proceedings could be initiated (triggered) by the Department of Commerce. Despite its initial theoretical elegance, the system collapsed of its own complexity and the inherent difficulty of enforcement.

TROPICAL PRODUCTS - Agricultural and other goods which are indigenous to tropical climates. The WTO uses this term to describe seven groups of products: tropical beverages (coffee, cocoa, tea, etc.); spices and cut flowers; oilseeds and vegetable oil; rice and tropical roots such as manoic; tropical fruits and nuts; tropical wood and rubber; and jute and other hard fibers such as sisal. The WTO Agreement on Agriculture, which came into force on January 1, 1995, covers trade in tropical products.

U

UNDERTAKING - *See Suspension Agreement*

UNFAIR COMPETITION - Those international trade practices such as export subsidization, dumping, discriminatory shipping arrangements, bribery and boycotts which can cause trade to flow in directions where market forces would not normally lead it.

UNFAIR TRADE PRACTICE - In the context of U.S. trade legislation, any act, policy, or practice of a foreign government that (1) violates, is inconsistent with, or otherwise denies benefits to the U.S. under any trade agreement to which the United States is a party; or (2) is unjustifiable, unreasonable, or discriminatory and burdens or restricts United States commerce. *See Section 301 of the Trade Act of 1974, Appendix I*

UNILATERAL - Having to do with, or arising from, one party only. Sometimes a country's unilateral trade actions have negative effects on the trade of one or several other countries.

UNITED NATIONS CENTRE ON TRANSNATIONAL CORPORATIONS (UNCTC) - The specialized body created by the UN Economic and Social Council in 1974 to serve along with the Commission on Transnational Corporations (CTC) *(see entry)* as focal points within the UN Secretariat for all matters related to transnational corporations. The Centre acts as a secretariat to the CTC and its work includes assisting intergovernmental bodies in creating rules to govern interaction between transnational corporations and host governments, research on trends of international investment flows, and technical cooperation to aid developing countries in their dealings with transnational corporations.

UNITED NATIONS CODE OF CONDUCT FOR LINER CONFERENCES - Adopted in 1974, this U.N. code seeks to promote an equitable international shipping system for ship owners in both developed and developing countries. One provision of the code calls for shipping to be divided in shares of 40% for the country of origin, 40% for the country receiving the cargo, and 20% for third countries. The United States is not a contracting party.

UNITED NATIONS COMMISSION ON INTERNATIONAL TRADE LAW (UNCITRAL) - A specialized body of the United Nations established in 1966 to reduce barriers to international trade and promote the continued harmonization and unification of international trade law. It has since become the U.N.'s primary legal framework for international trade law. The Commission's functions include coordination of the work of organizations active in international trade law, promotion of wider participation in such organizations, and establishment of new conventions and other instruments relating to international trade law.

UNITED NATIONS CONFERENCE ON TRADE AND DEVELOPMENT (UNCTAD) - A quasi-autonomous body within the United Nations system intended to focus special attention on economic relations between developed and developing countries, with particular regard to measures that might be taken by developed countries to accelerate economic development in the developing countries. The conference was first convened in Geneva in 1964 and has met quadrennially since. UNCTAD IX met in Midrand, South Africa, in 1996 and launched the "Partnership for Growth and Development" program. UNCTAD committees meet several times each year between the major conferences; their work is supported by the permanent UNCTAD Secretariat based in Geneva.

UNITED NATIONS ENVIRONMENT PROGRAMME (UNEP) - A program of the United Nations, based on arrangements made during the 1972 Stockholm Conference on the Human

Environment. UNEP's mandate is to raise environmental awareness by enabling nations to improve their quality of life without compromising that of future generations. Apart from the small percentage of UNEP's funding that is part of the regular budget of the United Nations, all of UNEP's money comes from voluntary contributions.

UNITED NATIONS INDUSTRIAL DEVELOPMENT ORGANIZATION (UNIDO) - An agency of the United Nations established in 1966 to promote and accelerate the industrialization of developing countries and to coordinate United Nations activities in this field. Headquartered in Vienna, it provides a forum for consultations and negotiations between developed and developing countries concerning industrial development, and provides technical assistance to developing countries.

UNITED STATES TRADE REPRESENTATIVE (USTR) - The Cabinet-level U.S. official primarily responsible for U.S. international trade. The USTR position was first established in 1963 as the "Special Trade Representative" of the President, in an effort by Congress to provide a neutral party to superintend the Departments of State, Commerce, and Agriculture in trade matters. The USTR's influence, duties and staff have expanded considerably since the office was created. The USTR acts as chief trade advisor to the President, primary trade negotiator and policy coordinator for the nation, and the U.S. representative to all major international trade organizations.

UPSTREAM SUBSIDY - In U.S. countervailing duty practice, a subsidy bestowed on inputs that are subsequently incorporated into a final product which is exported to the United States. The Department of Commerce is required to include the amount of the competitive benefit to the downstream manufacturer in the amount of any countervailing duty imposed on the merchandise being investigated.

URUGUAY ROUND NEGOTIATIONS - A broad set of trade-liberalizing GATT negotiations, initiated in Punta del Este, Uruguay, in September 1986. The Uruguay Round's far-ranging negotiations covered trade in services, tariffs, non-tariff measures, agriculture, tropical products, safeguards *(see entry)*, subsidies and countervailing measures, GATT articles, dispute settlement, the functioning of the GATT system (FOGS), trade-related aspects of intellectual property protection (TRIPS) *(see entry)*, trade-related investment measures (TRIMS) *(see entry)*, natural-resource based-products, and textiles and clothing. The Uruguay Round officially ended on April 15, 1994, with the signing of the Marrakesh Protocol *(see entry)*. The WTO, which came into being on January 1, 1995, arose out of the Uruguay Round negotiations.

U.S. AGENCY FOR INTERNATIONAL DEVELOPMENT (AID) -The arm of the United States Government which carries out programs designed to help the people of friendly, less developed countries develop their human and economic resources, increase their productive capacities, and improve their quality of life. AID also seeks to help build institutions which will promote economic and political stability in friendly countries.

U.S. - CANADA FREE TRADE AGREEMENT - The free trade agreement signed by the President of the United States and the Prime Minister of Canada on January 2, 1988. Implemented on January 1,1989, the agreement aimed to eliminate all tariff barriers between the two nations over a 10-year period. Subsequently, NAFTA superseded the FTA. *(See North America Free Trade Agreement)*

U.S. DEPARTMENT OF COMMERCE (DOC or USDOC) - A U.S. Government agency that promotes the nation's international trade, economic growth and technological advancement; and encourages the competitive free enterprise system. The DOC offers assistance and information to increase America's competitiveness in the world economy; administers programs to prevent unfair foreign trade competition; manages U.S. export controls; provides social and economic statistics and analyses for business and government planners; grants patents; and registers trademarks.

U.S. EXPORT ADMINISTRATION ACT OF 1969 - *See Appendix IV*

U.S. EXPORT ADMINISTRATION ACT OF 1979 - *See Appendix IV*

U.S. - ISRAEL FREE TRADE AGREEMENT - The 1985 free trade agreement between the United States and Israel. This agreement provided for the reciprocal elimination of tariffs on all traded goods between the U.S. and Israel by January 1, 1995 along with the elimination of certain other restrictions on bilateral trade.

U.S. PRICE - In the context of U.S. antidumping investigations, the price at which goods are sold in the United States. After appropriate adjustments, the U.S. price is compared to the export price or third country price of a good to determine the existence and magnitude of dumping margins.

USER FEE - A fee assessed by a government entity for a service it provides. Examples: charges for testing products; tolls for the use of bridges. Under GATT Article VIII, user fees are to be based on the estimated or actual cost of the service. A United States measure imposing a user fee for customs processing of import transactions was found by a GATT panel to be inconsistent with GATT because it was too high: the 0.17% fee exceeded the cost of the "service" involved.

V

VALUATION - The process of appraising imported goods for the assessment of duties. As a result of the Tokyo Round, many countries including the United States shifted to a method of valuation based primarily on transaction value. *See Transaction Value*

VALUE ADDED TAX (VAT or TVA) - An indirect tax assessed on the increase in the value of goods each time they change hands, from the raw material stage through the production process to final sale for consumption. The tax to each processor or merchant is levied on the value added -- the amount by which the processor or merchant has increased the value of the item sold. Under international trade rules, an indirect tax such as the VAT may be applied to imports and rebated upon exportation. *See Border Tax Adjustment*

VARIABLE LEVY - A tariff subject to change as world market prices change, the alterations being designed to assure that a product's import price after payment of duty will equal a predetermined "gate" price. The variable levy of the European Union — the best known example — equals the difference between the target price set by the EU for domestic agricultural products and the lowest offers for imported commodities on a CIF basis *(see entry)*. The amount of the levy is adjusted frequently to reflect changes in world market prices.

VISA SYSTEM - In the context of international trade in textiles, a method of tracking and controlling the quantity of textile products exported to the United States. This system monitors compliance with levels agreed upon in bilateral agreements or consultations. *See Textile Visa*

VISEGRAD GROUP - *See Central European Free Trade Agreement*

VOLUNTARY EXPORT RESTRAINT (VER) - A governmentally imposed unilateral restriction on exports. VERs usually do not entail formal agreements, but the export restrictions are generally undertaken to avoid the imposition of quotas or tariffs by the importing country. Japan's export restrictions on cars in the 1980's were VERs. *See Voluntary Restraint Agreement*

VOLUNTARY RESTRAINT AGREEMENT (VRA) - A bilateral arrangement in which an exporting country agrees to reduce or restrict exports. These agreements are generally undertaken to avoid action (such as quotas or tariffs) by an importing country wishing to limit imports that may injure or threaten domestic firms in the industry in question. Examples include agreements limiting steel exports to the U.S. and the EU in the 1980's. VRAs normally involve formal bilateral agreements; voluntary export restraints (VERs) generally are undertaken unilaterally. In either case, pressure may be applied by an importing country, giving rise to skepticism about the "voluntary" nature of such arrangements. VRA's and other "grey area" measures were effectively prohibited by the WTO Agreement on Safeguards.

W

WAIVER - In the context of international trade, a legal exception, provided for in Article XXV of GATT 1994, whereby the Members may, by a two-thirds vote, allow a signatory to maintain a practice that would otherwise violate its obligations. *See Section 22 in Appendix I*

WASSENAAR ARRANGEMENT - The shorthand term for the Wassenaar Arrangement on Export Controls for Conventional Arms and Dual-Use Goods and Technologies. The Wassenaar Arrangement was drawn up by representatives of 33 countries in Vienna, Austria in July 1996. The Arrangement's implementation procedures replaced those of COCOM *(see entry)*, but the Arrangement lacks the authority that COCOM wielded over its members. The control lists which were governed by COCOM, the List of Dual-Use Goods and Technologies, and the Munitions List *(see entry)* are also governed by the Wassenaar Arrangement.

WEBB-POMERENE ACT - The U.S. antitrust law, enacted in 1918, which provides a limited antitrust exemption for the formation and operation of corporations which normally compete with one another, to act collectively in export sales. This exemption is applicable to exporters only insofar as their actions do not negatively impact markets within the United States. This law offers no immunity from prosecution under foreign antitrust laws. *See Sherman Act*

WORLD BANK - A group of three international institutions -- the International Bank for Reconstruction and Development (IBRD), the International Finance Corporation (IFC) and the International Development Association (IDA) *(see entries)* -- which have the common objective of raising standards of living in developing countries. Sometimes the IBRD alone is referred to as the World Bank.

WORLD CUSTOMS ORGANIZATION (WCO) - An international body located in Brussels and also known as the Customs Cooperation Council, designed to foster cooperation in customs matters and to examine technical aspects of customs work, with a view to attaining the highest possible degree of uniformity in the customs practices of its member states. The activities of the WCO include drawing up, and ensuring uniform interpretation and application of, customs conventions on valuation, tariff and statistical nomenclature, and customs procedures; conciliatory action in disputes; circulation of information and advice regarding customs regulations and procedures; and cooperation with other international organizations.

WORLD HEALTH ORGANIZATION (WHO) - A specialized agency of the United Nations which sets standards for drugs, vaccines, and other substances affecting health. The WHO was established in July, 1946, with the U.S. a founding member. WHO headquarters are in Geneva, Switzerland.

WORLD INTELLECTUAL PROPERTY ORGANIZATION (WIPO) - One of the 15 "specialized agencies" of the United Nations system of organizations. WIPO, located in Geneva, promotes protection of intellectual property (copyrights, trademarks, patents) throughout the world through cooperation among states, and for the administration of various "unions," each founded on a multilateral treaty and dealing with the legal and administrative aspects of intellectual property. *See Berne Convention, Madrid Arrangement, Paris Convention, Uruguay Round Negotiations*

WORLD TRADE ORGANIZATION (WTO) - The global body established in 1995 at the conclusion of the Uruguay Round of Multilateral Trade Negotiations to provide the common institutional framework for the conduct of trade relations among its Members. The WTO 1) facilitates the implementation, administration, and operation of Members' multilateral and plurilateral trade agreements; 2) provides a forum for negotiations among its members concerning their multilateral trade relations; 3) administers the Understanding on Rules and Procedures Governing the Settlement of Disputes; 4) administers the Trade Policy Review Mechanism; and 5) cooperates with the IMF and IBRD and their affiliated agencies. The WTO is governed by its highest authority, the Ministerial Conference, composed of representatives of all WTO Members. The day-to-day work of the WTO falls to a number of subsidiary bodies, principally the General Council.

WTO GENERAL COUNCIL - The working arm of the WTO, operating under the authority of the Ministerial Conference, which meets every two years. The General Council and Ministerial Conference consist of representatives of all WTO Members. The members of the General Council also serve as members of the Dispute Settlement Body and the Trade Policy Review Board. Only the Ministerial Conference and the General Council have the authority to interpret the WTO Agreements, amend the Agreements, and grant waivers of obligations. All accessions to the WTO must be approved by the General Council acting on behalf of the Ministerial Conference. Three major sectoral bodies report to the General Council: the Council for Trade in Goods, the Council for Trade in Services, and the Council for Trade-Related Aspects of Intellectual Property Protection (TRIPS).

WTO SECRETARIAT - Located in Geneva, Switzerland, this is the WTO's executive and administrative body. It has approximately 450 staff members headed by a Director-General and four Deputy Directors-General. Its responsibilities include the servicing of WTO delegate bodies with respect to negotiations and the implementation of agreements. It has a particular responsibility to provide technical support to developing countries, in particular least developed countries. WTO economists and statisticians provide trade performance and trade policy analyses while members of the WTO's legal staff assist in resolution of trade disputes involving the interpretation of WTO rules and precedents. The Secretariat's work also includes accession negotiations for new members, and providing advice to governments considering membership.

X, Y, Z

YAOUNDE AGREEMENTS - Agreements signed between members of the European Union and former French, Belgian, Dutch and Italian colonies which wanted to continue economic relationships after their independence. Yaounde I was signed in 1963 and Yaounde II in 1969. The Lome Convention replaced the Yaounde Agreements in 1973. *Syn. Yaounde Convention*

YELLOW SUBSIDY - *See Actionable Subsidy*

YEN BLOCK - An informal term referring to Japan, Australia, Hong Kong, Korea, New Zealand, and the member nations of ASEAN; and to the economic relationships among them.

YEN DIPLOMACY - A pejorative reference to alleged attempts by Japan to use its economic power to create and control trade relationships among Pacific Rim nations.

ZAIBATSU - *See Keiretsu*

APPENDIX I

AN OUTLINE OF THE WORLD TRADE AGREEMENT
(establishing the WTO and including GATT 1994)

The Final Act and Agreement Establishing the World Trade Organization (including GATT 1994), Uruguay Round; Marrakesh, April 15, 1994.

I. FINAL ACT

II. AGREEMENT ESTABLISHING THE WORLD TRADE ORGANIZATION

ANNEX 1A: Multilateral Agreements on Trade in Goods
The following Agreements, understandings and decisions are an integral part of the Uruguay Round Agreements:

1. General Agreement on Tariffs and Trade 1994:

(a) The provisions in the General Agreement on Tariffs and Trade, dated October 30, 1947.

(b) The provisions of the legal instruments set forth below that have entered into force under the GATT 1947 before the date of entry into force of the WTO Agreement:

(i) protocols and certifications relating to tariff

concessions;

(ii) protocols of accession;

(iii) decisions on waivers granted under Article XXV of GATT 1947;

(iv) other decisions of the CONTRACTING PARTIES to GATT 1947.

(c) The understandings set forth below:

(i) Understanding on the Interpretation of Article II: l(b) (Tariff Binding);

(ii) Understanding on the Interpretation of Article XVII (State Trading);

(iii) Understanding on Balance-of-Payments Provisions;

(iv) Understanding on the Interpretation of Article XXIV (Customs Union and Free Trade Areas);

(v) Understanding in Respect of Waivers of Obligations;

(vi) Understanding on the Interpretation of Article XXVIII (Tariff Modification).

(d) The Marrakesh Protocol to GATT 1994.

2. Agreement on Agriculture

3. Agreement on the Application of Sanitary and Phytosanitary Measures

4. Agreement on Textiles and Clothing

5. Agreement on Technical Barriers to Trade

6. Agreement on Trade-Related Investment Measures

7. Agreement on Implementation of Article VI of the GATT 1994

8. Agreement on Implementation of Article VII of the GATT 1994

9. Agreement on Preshipment Inspection

10. Agreement on Rules of Origin

11. Agreement on Import Licensing Procedures

12. Agreement on Subsidies and Countervailing Measures

13. Agreement on Safeguards

ANNEX 1B: General Agreement on Trade in Services, and Annexes

ANNEX 1C: Agreement on Trade-Related Aspects of Intellectual Property Rights, Including trade in counterfeit goods

ANNEX 2: Understanding on Rules and Procedures Governing the Settlement of Disputes

ANNEX 3: Trade Policy Review Mechanism

ANNEX 4: Plurilateral Trade Agreements:

(a) Agreement on Trade in Civil Aircraft

(b) Agreement on Government Procurement

(c) International Dairy Arrangement

(d) Arrangement Regarding Bovine Meat

III. MINISTERIAL DECISIONS AND DECLARATIONS

1. Decision on Measures in Favor of Least-Developed Countries

2. Declaration on the Contribution of the WTO to Achieving Greater Coherence in Global Economic Policymaking

3. Decision on Notification Procedures

4. Customs Valuation:

    (a) Decision Regarding Cases where Customs Administrations Have Reasons to Doubt the Truth or Accuracy of the Declared Value

    (b) Texts Relating to Minimum Values and Imports by Sole Agents, Sole Distributors and Sole Concessionaires

5. Technical Barriers to Trade:

    (a) Proposed Understanding on WTO-ISO Standards Information System

    (b) Decision on Review of the ISO/IEC Information Centre Publications

6. Decision on Measures Concerning the Possible Negative Effects of the Reform Programme on Least-Developed and Net Food-Importing Developing Countries

7. General Agreement on Trade in Services:

    (a) Decision on Institutional Arrangements for the General Agreement on Trade in Services
    (b) Decision on Certain Dispute Settlement Procedures for the General Agreement on Trade in Services

(c) Decision concerning Paragraph (b) of Article XIV

(d) Decision on Negotiations on Basic Telecommunications

(e) Understanding on Commitments in Financial Services

(f) Decision on Financial Services

(g) Decision concerning Professional Services

(h) Decision on Movement of Natural Persons

8. Decision on Implementation of Article XXIV:2 of the Agreement on Government Procurement

9. Decision on the Application and Review of the Understanding on Rules and Procedures Governing the Settlement of Disputes

10. Decision on Improvements to the GATT Dispute Settlement Rules and Procedures

11. Agreement on Implementation of Article VI of GATT 1994

(a) Decision on Anti-Circumvention

(b) Decision on Standard of Review for Dispute Settlement Panels

12. Decision on Dispute Settlement pursuant to the Agreement on Implementation of Article VI of GATT 1994 or Part V of the Agreement on Subsidies and Countervailing Measures 1994

APPENDIX II

WTO MEMBERS

(134 Members as of February 28, 1999)

Members	Entry into Force
Angola	December 1, 1996
Antigua/Barbuda	January 1, 1995
Argentina	January 1, 1995
Australia	January 1, 1995
Austria	January 1, 1995
Bahrain	January 1, 1995
Bangladesh	January 1, 1995
Barbados	January 1, 1995
Belgium	January 1, 1995
Belize	January 1, 1995
Benin	February 22, 1996
Bolivia	September 13, 1995
Botswana	May 31, 1995
Brazil	January 1, 1995
Brunei Darussalam	January 1, 1995
Bulgaria	December 1, 1996
Burkina Faso	June 3, 1995
Burma	January 1, 1995
Burundi	July 23, 1995
Cameroon	December 13, 1995
Canada	January 1, 1995
Central African Republic	May 31, 1995
Chad	October 19, 1996

Members	Entry into Force
Chile	January 1, 1995
Colombia	April 30, 1995
Congo	March 27, 1997
Costa Rica	January 1, 1995
Cote D'Ivoire	January 1, 1995
Cuba	April 20, 1995
Cyprus	July 30, 1995
Czech Republic	January 1, 1995
Democratic Republic of the Congo	January 1, 1997
Denmark	January 1, 1995
Djibouti	May 31, 1995
Dominica	January 1, 1995
Dominican Republic	March 9, 1995
Ecuador	January 21, 1996
Egypt	June 30 1995
El Salvador	May 7, 1995
European Union	January 1, 1995
Fiji	January 14, 196
Finland	January 1, 1995
France	January 1, 1995
Gabon	January 1, 1995
Gambia	October 23, 1996
Germany	January 1, 1995
Ghana	January 1, 1995
Greece	January 1, 1995
Grenada	February 22, 1996
Guatemala	July 21, 1995
Guinea	October 25, 1995
Guinea Bissau	May 31, 1995
Guyana	January 1, 1995
Haiti	January 30, 1996
Honduras	January 1, 1995
Hong Kong, China	January 1, 1995
Hungary	January 1, 1995
Iceland	January 1, 1995

Members	Entry into Force
India	January 1, 1995
Indonesia	January 1, 1995
Ireland	January 1, 1995
Israel	April 21, 1995
Italy	January 1, 1995
Jamaica	March 9, 1995
Japan	January 1, 1995
Kenya	January 1, 1995
Korea	January 1, 1995
Kuwait	January 1, 1995
Kyrgyz Republic	December 20, 1998
Latvia	February 10, 1999
Lesotho	May 31, 1995
Liechtenstein	September 1, 1995
Luxembourg	January 1, 1995
Macau	January 1, 1995
Madagascar	November 17, 1995
Malawi	May 31, 1995
Malaysia	January 1, 1995
Maldives	May 31, 1995
Mali	May 31, 1995
Malta	January 1, 1995
Mauritania	May 31, 1995
Mauritius	January 1, 1995
Mexico	January 1, 1995
Mongolia	January 29, 1997
Morocco	January 1, 1995
Mozambique	August 26, 1995
Namibia	January 1, 1995
Netherlands - for the Kingdom in Europe and for the Netherlands Antillies	January 1, 1995
New Zealand	January 1, 1995
Nicaragua	September 3, 1995
Niger	December 13, 1995

Members	Entry into Force
Nigeria	January 1, 1995
Norway	January 1, 1995
Pakistan	January 1, 1995
Panama	September 6, 1997
Papua New Guinea	June 9, 1996
Paraguay	January 1, 1995
Peru	January 1, 1995
Philippines	January 1, 1995
Poland	July 1, 1995
Portugal	January 1, 1995
Qatar	January 13, 1996
Romania	January 1, 1995
Rwanda	May 22, 1996
St. Kitts and Nevis	February 21, 1996
St. Lucia	January 1, 1995
St. Vincent & Grenadines	January 1, 1995
Senegal	January 1, 1995
Sierra Leone	July 23, 1995
Singapore	January 1, 1995
Slovak Republic	January 1, 1995
Slovenia	July 30, 1995
Solomon Islands	July 26, 1996
South Africa	January 1, 1995
Spain	January 1, 1995
Sri Lanka	January 1, 1995
Suriname	January 1, 1995
Swaziland	January 1, 1995
Sweden	January 1, 1995
Switzerland	July 1, 1995
Tanzania	January 1, 1995
Thailand	January 1, 1995
Togo	May 31, 1995
Trinidad & Tobago	March 1, 1995
Tunisia	March 29, 1995
Turkey	March 26, 1995
Uganda	January 1, 1995

Members	Entry into Force
United Arab Emirates	April 10, 1996
United States	January 1, 1995
Uruguay	January 1, 1995
Venezuela	January 1, 1995
Zambia	January 1, 1995
Zimbabwe	March 3, 1995

WTO Observer Governments (34)

Albania
Algeria
Andorra
Armenia
Azerbaijan
Belarus
Bhutan
Cambodia
Cape Verde
China
Chinese Taipei
Croatia
Estonia
Ethiopia
Former Yugoslav Republic of Macedonia
Georgia
Holy See (Vatican)
Jordan
Kazakstan
Laos
Lithuania
Moldova
Nepal
Oman
Russian Federation
Samoa
Saudi Arabia
Seychelles
Sudan
Tonga
Ukraine
Uzbekistan
Vanuata
Vietnam

Note: *All observer countries have applied to join the WTO except the Holy See (Vatican) and, for the time being, Ethiopia, Bhutan, and Cape Verde.*

International organization observers to General Council
(observers in other councils and committees differ)

United Nations (UN)
United Nations Conference on Trade and Development (UNCTAD)
International Monetary Fund (IMF)
International Bank for Reconstruction and Development (World Bank)
Food and Agricultural Organization (FAO)
World Intellectual Property Organization (WIPO)
Organization for Economic Cooperation and Development (OECD)

APPENDIX III

GATT ROUNDS

Listed below are the sets of international trade negotiations conducted under the auspices of the General Agreement on Tariffs and Trade. Eight rounds have been completed since the GATT was established in 1947.

1947 - 1st Round (Geneva, Switzerland). The first round of trade negotiations actually took place simultaneously with the GATT's creation. Negotiations were carried out mainly on a product-by-product, bilateral basis, and agreed-upon concessions were later extended to other nations under the most-favored-nation (MFN) principle. Twenty-three members participated.

1949 - 2nd Round (Annecy, France). During the Annecy Round, 10 more countries acceded to GATT, bringing its membership to 33 countries.

1951 - 3rd Round (Torquay, England). During the third round of negotiations, GATT membership rose to 37 countries.

1956 - 4th Round (Geneva, Switzerland). Significant tariff reductions were negotiated in this round. The fourth round was particularly important because of the Haberler Report, which first set guidelines for addressing the trade and development needs of developing countries, and for dealing with the effects of agricultural protectionism in industrial economies. The report was prepared by a panel of experts led by Gottfried Haberler, a professor of economics at Harvard University.

1960-1962 - The Dillon Round (Geneva, Switzerland). As previously, negotiations in the Dillon Round were carried out mostly on a product-by-product basis. Tariff concessions covering $4.9 billion of trade were negotiated by the participating members. In this round it became evident that future negotiations would need to focus on non-tariff as well as tariff barriers, and on the problems of trade in agricultural products.

1964-1967 - The Kennedy Round (Geneva, Switzerland). Forty-eight countries participated in this sixth round of multilateral trade negotiations. The developing countries played a more important role in the Kennedy Round and benefited from the concessions of the then-new Part IV of the GATT. Negotiations for cutting tariffs were, for the first time, carried out largely on an across-the-board, or linear, basis, and covered $40 billion in trade. An agreement was concluded on antidumping, but the U.S. Congress refused to implement it.

1973-1979 - The Tokyo Round (Geneva, Switzerland). Ninety-nine member and non-member countries negotiated in this seventh round. For the first time, non-tariff barriers were a central focus of the negotiations, resulting in codes on antidumping, customs valuation, government procurement, and subsidies and countervailing measures. In addition, tariff reductions covering $300 billion of trade were agreed upon. The large industrial countries' average tariff on manufactured goods fell from 7% to 4.7%. *See Tokyo Round Negotiations*

1986-1994 - The Uruguay Round (Geneva, Switzerland). In Punta del Este, Uruguay, 117 countries launched a new round of trade negotiations aimed at reducing tariffs worldwide and at expanding the scope of international rules concerning agriculture, services, intellectual property and investment. This round made considerable progress in revising existing antidumping and subsidy rules; instituting both a dispute settlement mechanism and a trade policy mechanism; establishing the World Trade Organization (WTO); and consolidating the requirements of the GATT system so that, for the most part, all Members of the WTO have similar obligations. *See Uruguay Round Negotiations*, *World Trade Organization*

APPENDIX IV

MAJOR U.S. TRADE POLICY LEGISLATION

ANTIDUMPING ACT OF 1916 (15 U.S.C. 71 et seq.) - The first U.S. antidumping statute. It allows action in federal court for private damages and criminal penalties. Suits may be filed against importers, or those who assist the importation, of articles sold at prices substantially below their wholesale prices or actual market value in the home market, with the intent of destroying or injuring a U.S. industry. The legislation's status under the WTO is a source of controversy.

EXPORT TRADING COMPANY ACT (15 U.S.C 4001 et seq.) - The 1982 act established for the purpose of increasing U.S. exports of products and services by encouraging more efficient provision of export trade services to U.S. producers and suppliers, particularly small and medium-sized firms.

OMNIBUS TRADE AND COMPETITIVENESS ACT OF 1988 (codified as amended at various sections of Title XIX and several other Titles, P.L. 100-418) - An act designed to increase the emphasis placed on trade and other international economic policy interests within the U.S. Government. The act gives trade negotiators leverage to seek liberalization of foreign trade barriers, and increases Presidential power to impose import restrictions on products of foreign countries whose trade actions the President deems unfair. The act requires the U.S. Government to identify countries that engage in unfair trade practices, negotiate with those countries, and retaliate against them if no corrective measures are taken. Additionally, the act is designed to strengthen U.S. competitiveness through research and technological development. Finally, the act revised various U.S. trade laws (e.g., the countervailing duty and anti-dumping statutes, the Export Administration Act of 1979, and Section 301 of the Trade Act of 1974).

RECIPROCAL TRADE AGREEMENTS ACT OF 1934 (19 U.S.C. 1001, 1201, 1351, 1354; P.L. 73-316) - A U.S. law which before World War II provided authority for the U.S. Government to enter into bilateral agreements with other countries for reciprocal tariff reductions which were then extended to other countries through most-favored-nation clauses. It also provided the authority for U.S. participation in the first five rounds of GATT trade negotiations from 1947 through the Dillon Round (1960-62). It was superseded by the Trade Expansion Act of 1962, which in turn was superseded by the Trade Act of 1974. *See Most-Favored-Nation Treatment.*

SECTION 22 - The section of the U.S. Agriculture Adjustment Act of 1933 (7 U.S.C. 601 et. seq.) that requires the President to limit imports of farm products that "are being, or are practically certain to be, imported into the United States under such conditions and in such quantities as to render or tend to render ineffective, or materially interfere with" any U.S. farm program. Section 22 is the subject of a 1955 GATT decision that waived indefinitely, subject to annual reviews, the rights of GATT signatories that would otherwise be violated by the import restrictions imposed under the authority of this provision.

In the Uruguay Round's Agreement on Agriculture, the U.S. agreed to change all quotas and fees on imports into tariff quotas for WTO members. Since this agreement, Section 22 restrictions may only be imposed on imports from countries outside the WTO.

SECTION 201 (19 U.S.C. 2251 et seq.) - The provision of the U.S. Trade Act of 1974 (19 U.S.C. 2251 et seq., P.L. 93-618) which requires the U.S. International Trade Commission to investigate petitions filed by domestic industries or workers claiming serious injury or threat thereof due to increased imports. If such injury is found, temporary measures to restrict imports may be taken. Import restrictions under Section 201 do not require a showing of any unfair trade practice, like dumping, by foreign firms or governments. Action under Section 201 is allowed under GATT Article XIX, the escape clause *(see entry)*.

SECTION 232 (19 U.S.C. 1862, 1864) - The provision of the Trade Expansion Act of 1962 (19 U.S.C. 1862, 1864, P.L. 87-794) as amended, under which the U.S. Department of Commerce determines whether articles are being imported into the U.S. in quantities or circumstances that threaten national security. Commerce must report to the President on the effects the imports have on national security, and make recommendations for action or inaction, within 270 days of starting an investigation. Within 90 days of receiving the report, the President must decide whether to take action to adjust imports on the basis of national security. The President then must notify Congress of his decision within 30 days. *See Trade Expansion Act of 1962*

SECTION 301 - The provision of the U.S. Trade Act of 1974 (19 U.S.C. 2411-2420, P.L. 93-618) *(see entry)* designed to eliminate unfair foreign government trade practices (other than subsidization) that adversely affect U.S. trade or investment. The provision's scope includes both goods and services. Under Section 301, as modified by Sections 1301-1303 of the Omnibus Trade and Competitiveness Act of 1988 *(see entry),* the USTR must determine whether the practices in question are unjustifiable, unreasonable or discriminatory, and whether they burden or restrict U.S. commerce. The amended law directs the USTR to take all appropriate and feasible action to secure the elimination of the offending practice(s), unless otherwise directed by the President. *See Special 301, Super 301*

SECTION 302 - The section of the NAFTA Implementation Act (19 U.S.C. 3352, P.L. 103-182) which stipulates that the U.S. International Trade Commission (USITC) *(see entry)* must determine whether increased imports from Canada or Mexico, resulting from decreased or eliminated duties under NAFTA, are a substantial cause of serious injury, or threat of serious injury, to a U.S. industry. If its determination is affirmative, the ITC recommends a remedy to the President. Section 302 investigations proceed much like those under Section 201 of the U.S. Trade Act of 1974 *(see entry)*.

SECTION 332 (19 U.S.C. 1332) - The provision of the Tariff Act of 1930 (P.L. 71-361) that authorizes the U.S. International Trade Commission (formerly the U.S. Tariff Commission) to conduct studies on any issues involving tariffs and international trade, on the ITC's own initiative or at the request of the President, the USTR, the Senate Finance Committee, or the House Ways and Means Committee. These investigations sometimes give rise to unfair trade cases (e.g., antidumping, countervailing duty and Section 301 cases).

SECTION 337 (19 U.S.C. 1337) - The provision of the Tariff Act of 1930 (P.L. 71-361) which empowers the International Trade Commission (ITC) *(see entry),* subject to override by the President, to prohibit importation of goods involved in unfair trade practices. Most investigations of this nature focus on violations of U.S. patent, copyright or trademark rights or violations concerning the "misappropriation of trade secrets." This section is heavily utilized by the technology sector.

SECTION 406 (19 U.S.C. 2436) - The section of the U.S. Trade Act of 1974 that permits the President to restrict imports of any product from most non-market economy countries, if the U.S. International Trade Commission finds that imports of the product are causing or threatening disruption of the U.S. market for the product. These investigations proceed similarly to those under Section 201. If the ITC determines that there is market disruption, it submits a remedy recommendation to the President, who decides on any final action. *See Market Disruption, Jackson-Vanik Amendment*

SECTION 592 (19 U.S.C. 1592) - Section 592 of the U.S. Tariff Act of 1930, as amended, the most widely used customs penalty provision. Under this law, civil monetary penalties may be imposed on any person using false documents, statements, or practices when importing, attempting to import, or aiding in the importation of merchandise. Persons who present false documentation to customs officers may be punished by up to 2 years imprisonment, a $5000 fine, or both.

SMOOT-HAWLEY ACT - *See U.S. Tariff Act of 1930*

SPECIAL 301 (P.L. 100-418) - A distinct part of Section 301 of the 1988 U.S. Omnibus Trade and Competitiveness Act, Special 301 requires the U.S. Trade Representative to identify nations which fail to protect intellectual property rights of U.S. firms. After identifying a problem, the USTR has six months to resolve it through negotiations with the offending country; if negotiations fail, the USTR must take retaliatory measures.

SUPER 301 (P.L. 100-418) - Section 301 of the Trade Act of 1974, as re-written in the 1988 U.S. Omnibus Trade and Competitiveness Act. Super 301 requires the U.S. Trade Representative to identify nations that conduct unfair trade practices and seek to engage those countries in negotiations to end the objectionable practices. If no agreement is achieved within 18 months, the USTR is required to retaliate against the offending nations.

U.S. EXPORT ADMINISTRATION ACT OF 1969 (50 U.S.C. 2401 et seq.) - Legislation which provided authority for the President to limit or suspend exports of U.S. commodities and technical data to foreign destinations for any of three specified purposes: to protect the national security, to ensure against an excessive drain of scarce goods, or to further foreign policy objectives. Replaced by the U.S. Export Administration Act of 1979 *(see entry).*

U.S. EXPORT ADMINISTRATION ACT OF 1979 (50 App. U.S.C. 2401-2420, P.L. 96-72) - Legislation which expanded the provisions of the U.S. Export Administration Act of 1969 to include detailed procedures for monitoring and restricting exports for reasons of national security and foreign policy. A "military critical technologies list" (MCTL) was created as a more specialized version of the Commercial Control List (CCL) *(see entry).* The Act also officially authorized U.S. participation in the Coordinating Committee on Multilateral Export Controls (CoCom) *(see entry).* The Act expired in March 1984 and was re-authorized for four years in July 1985 by the Export Administration Amendments Act of 1985. The Omnibus Trade and Competitiveness Act of 1988 substantially revised and broadened the provisions of this law.

U.S. TARIFF ACT OF 1930 (codified as amended at various sections of Titles VI, XIX, and XXII; P.L. 71-361) - The Smoot-Hawley Act. This broad trade legislation is best known for representing the peak of an extremely protectionist era in U.S. economic policy. Under Smoot-Hawley, tariffs reached an average rate of 53 percent on dutiable imports. The law provoked retaliatory tariff increases by other countries, resulting in worldwide escalation of tariffs and, in the view of many economists, contributing to the world depression of the 1930s. Although almost all U.S. column 1 *(see entry)* tariffs have been reduced to a small fraction of their Smoot-Hawley levels (with many eliminated altogether), the Smoot-Hawley rates survive as the column 2 rates *(see entry)*.

Of particular note is the current version of Title VII of this law, which provides for the imposition of antidumping duties on imported merchandise found to have been sold in the United States at "less than fair value," *(see entry)* if these sales have caused or are likely to cause material injury to, or materially retard the establishment of, an industry in the United States.

U.S. TRADE ACT OF 1974 (codified as amended at various sections of Titles V, XIX, XXVI, and XXXI; P.L. 93-618) - U.S. legislation signed in January 1975 that granted the President broad authority to enter into international agreements to reduce import barriers. The stated purposes of the act were "to stimulate the economic growth of the United States and to maintain and enlarge foreign markets for the products of U.S. agriculture, industry, mining and commerce; to strengthen economic relations with other countries through the development of open and non-discriminatory trading in the free world; to provide adequate procedures to safeguard American industry and American workers against unfair or injurious import competition; and to provide adjustment assistance to industries, workers, and communities injured or threatened by increased import competition." The Trade Act also granted the President authority to extend tariff preferences to certain imports from developing countries *(see Generalized System of Preferences)*, and it set conditions under which MFN treatment could be extended to imports from non-market economy countries. *See Jackson-Vanik Amendment*

U.S. TRADE AGREEMENTS ACT OF 1979 (codified as amended at various sections of Titles V, XIII, XIX, and XXVIII; P.L. 96-39) - The U.S. Trade Agreements Acts of 1979 approved and implemented the trade agreements negotiated by the United States, under the Trade Act of 1974, in the Tokyo Round of Multilateral Trade Negotiations. The act incorporated into U.S. law the Tokyo Round agreements on countervailing and anti-dumping duties, customs valuation, government procurement, product standards, and civil aircraft. The act also approved the newly negotiated arrangements on trade in meat and dairy products, and a new system for liquor duties. The act also extended the President's authority to negotiate trade agreements with foreign countries and reduce or eliminate non-tariff barriers, and it required the President to reorganize executive agency trade functions and responsibilities. U.S. obligations under the Uruguay Round Agreement on Technical Barriers and the NAFTA have been implemented through amendments to Titles III and IV of this act.

U.S. TRADE AND TARIFF ACT OF 1984 (P.L. 98-573) - U.S. trade legislation amending the countervailing duty and antidumping laws and clarifying the conditions under which unfair trade cases may be pursued under Section 301 of the Trade Act of 1974. It also provided enforcement authority for voluntary restraint agreements on steel, negotiating authority for the U.S.-Israel Free Trade Agreement, and procedures to be followed for congressional approval of future bilateral agreements.

U.S. TRADE EXPANSION ACT OF 1962 (codified as amended at various sections of Title XIX; P.L. 87-573) - The legislative authority for U.S. participation in the Kennedy Round of trade negotiations. The act also authorized the Adjustment Assistance Program and the appointment of a Special Representative for Trade Negotiations (now the United States Trade Representative). Section 232 of this act authorizes the President to impose, in certain circumstances and subject to Congressional override, restrictions on imports which he deems detrimental to national security. *See Section 232*

URUGUAY ROUND AGREEMENTS ACT (codified as amended at various sections of Title XIX and several other titles; P.L. 103-465) - U.S. legislation introduced in order to implement the Uruguay Round Agreements.

APPENDIX V

ANTIDUMPING AND COUNTERVAILING DUTY INVESTIGATION TIMETABLES

I. TIMETABLE FOR ANTIDUMPING DUTY INVESTIGATIONS

DAY	STEPS
0	Filing of petition with International Trade Commission (ITC) and the Department of Commerce (DOC)
20[1]	Initiation of investigation
45	ITC Preliminary Determination[5]
160[2]	DOC Preliminary Determination
235[3]	DOC Final Determination[5]
280[4]	ITC Final Determination [5]

[1]Initiation may be extended by up to 20 days if additional industry support needs to be determined. This extension increases the length of all other subsequent deadlines by the amount of the extension.
[2] In complicated cases, the DOC may have up to an additional 50 days to complete its preliminary determination.
[3] May be extended for up to 60 days.
[4] If the DOC's preliminary determination is negative, the ITC's final determination deadline may be extended by up to an additional 30 days from the DOC final determination.
[5] A negative determination at this stage terminates the proceeding

ANTIDUMPING AND COUNTERVAILING DUTY INVESTIGATION TIMETABLES

II. TIMETABLE FOR COUNTERVAILING DUTY INVESTIGATIONS

DAY	STEPS
0	Filing of petition with International Trade Commission (ITC) and Department of Commerce (DOC)
20[1]	Initiation of investigation
45	ITC Preliminary Determination[4]
85[2]	DOC Preliminary Determination
160	DOC Final Determination[4]
205[3]	ITC Final Determination[4]

[1] Initiation may be extended up to 40 days if additional industry support needs to be determined. This extension increases the length of all other subsequent deadlines by the amount of the extension.
[2] In complicated cases, the DOC may have up to an additional 65 days to complete its preliminary determination.
[3] If the DOC's preliminary determination is negative, the ITC's final determination deadline may be extended by up to an additional 30 days from the DOC final determination.
[4] A negative determination at this stage terminates the proceeding

APPENDIX VI

THE EUROPEAN UNION

In November 1993, the Maastricht Treaty on European Union entered into force creating the European Union (EU), a body of nations created by and from the member states of the European Community (EC), significantly broadening and deepening the integration of its members. While the founding treaties of the European Communities (Euratom, ECSC, and EEC) centered on economic integration, the EU is additionally a step toward monetary and political integration. The EU's current 15 members are Austria, Belgium, Denmark, Finland, France, Germany, Greece, Ireland, Italy, Luxembourg, the Netherlands, Portugal, Spain, Sweden, and the United Kingdom.

The structure of the EU is generally described as consisting of three pillars: (a) the European Community, ultimately including a single currency and European citizenship; (b) a Common Foreign and Security Policy; and (c) cooperation among member states in the fields of justice and home (internal) affairs.

The governing institutions of the EU have grown in both number and size since the inception of this union. Under the former European Community system, the European Commission proposed legislation, the European Parliament was consulted about it, the Council of Ministers enacted legislation based on the proposal, and the European Court of Justice interpreted it.

Today, the institutions governing the EU are as follows:

I. **The European Parliament** is the 626-member assembly of representatives of all EU citizens. Representatives are elected for five-year terms by direct universal suffrage and must be consulted on proposed EU legislation. The Parliament may amend proposals for legislation, veto the accession of a new member state, complete association agreements with third countries, and confirm or remove the appointment of the Commission, all of which give the Parliament extensive influence, if not control, over EU activities. Parliament jointly shares EU budgetary authority, including oversight powers, with the Council of Ministers. In this capacity, the Parliament has the final say over non-compulsory expenditures. However, the expenditures for agriculture, which account for over 50 percent of the EU budget, are compulsory; a large portion of the budget, therefore, is beyond the Parliament's control.

II. **The Council of the European Union** (Council, sometimes referred to as the Council of Ministers), assisted by the General Secretariat, holds ultimate legislative authority. The Council enacts EU laws and has the authority by unanimous agreement to change legislative proposals by the Commission. The Council is aided in its work by the Committee of Permanent Representatives (Coreper). The term "Council of Ministers" is applied to any meeting of member state cabinet ministers — ministers of agriculture, finance, industry, foreign affairs, etc. There are more than 25 different types of Council meetings. General Affairs (Foreign Affairs Ministers), Economy and Finance, and Agriculture meet monthly; other Ministerial Councils, such as Transport, Environment and Industry, meet two to four times a year. Each country of the EU in turn holds the chair, or presidency, for six months. Twice each year, the heads of government of the EU member states meet, together with the President of the Commission, as the "European Council."

III. **The European Commission** is the administrative arm of the EU. Except in areas of foreign and security policy, and justice and home affairs, the Commission has the sole power to initiate legislation. The Commission has investigative powers and may hold any person, company, or member state legally responsible for any violation of EU rules. Additionally, the Commission manages the EU budget and represents the Union in international trade negotiations. There are 20 Commissioners: two each from France, Germany, Italy, Spain, and the United Kingdom; and one from every other member state. Commissioners are appointed to serve five year terms.

IV. **The Court of Justice** together with the Court of First Instance make up the judicial branch of the EU. They decide challenges to actions by EU institutions and cases involving alleged infringements by member states of their obligations under EU law.

V. **The Court of Auditors** oversees all expenditures and has jurisdiction over the management of the EU budget. Based in Luxembourg, the Court's 15 members are appointed by the Council, subject to Parliamentary consultation, and serve six year terms.

VI. **Other Bodies of the EU** which are frequently consulted prior to the adoption of new legislation are the:

A. Economic and Social Committee (Brussels)
B. Committee of the Regions (Brussels)
C. European Investment Bank (Luxembourg)
D. Community Plant Variety Office (Brussels)
E. European Agency for Health and Safety at Work (Luxembourg)
F. European Agency for the Evaluation of Medicinal Products (London)
G. European Central Bank (Frankfurt)
H. European Environment Agency (Copenhagen)
I. European Monetary Institute (Frankfurt)
J. European Ombudsman (Brussels)
K. European Police Office (EUROPOL) (The Hague)
L. European Training Foundation (Turin)
M. Office for Harmonization in the Internal Market (Alicante)
N. Office for Veterinary and Plant Health Inspection and Control (Dublin)

Member States by Year of Accession

The EU's original six members, Belgium, France, Germany, Italy, Luxembourg, and the Netherlands established the European Economic Community in 1958. Four waves of accession have followed:

1973	Denmark, Ireland, and United Kingdom
1981	Greece
1986	Portugal and Spain
1995	Austria, Finland, and Sweden

Future Negotiations for Possible Accession

In accordance with its policy of enlargement, the EU anticipates more new members. Based on economic and political criteria, candidates for possible accession have been placed in two separate rounds for bilateral negotiations with the EU:

First Round:	Cyprus, Czech Republic, Estonia, Hungary, Poland, and Slovenia
Second Round:	Bulgaria, Latvia, Lithuania, Romania, and Slovakia

Any future negotiations with these countries will deal with the process by which the applicant countries will adopt and implement existing EU laws and standards, in accordance with the *aquis communautaire*.

Basic Economic Indicators:

The EU has become a formidable economic power by any measure:

Basic Statistics 1997

	EU	U.S.
Area (square miles)	1,249.0	3,732.4
Population (millions)	373.3	267.6
Population Density (persons/sq.mi.)	298.9	71.1
Unemployment Rate (%)	10.7	4.9
Gross Domestic Product (billions $)	8093.4	7819.3

World Trade 1997 Excluding Intra-EU Trade

Billions USD	EU	U.S.
Imports	756.8	870.7
Exports	814.1	689.2
Direct investment in the U.S.	381.9	—
Direct investment in the EU	—	369.0

Trade as a Percentage of GDP 1997

	EU	U.S.
Imports	9.4	11.5
Exports	9.1	8.8

APPENDIX VII

INCOTERMS

Incoterms comprise a standardized set of the most commonly used terms in international trade. The International Chamber of Commerce published the first set of Incoterms in 1936; the list below comes from the 1990 revision.

The terms have been grouped in four categories, according to the first letter of each term's three-letter designation. Terms begining with "C" refer to arrangements where a seller will contract for carriage without assuming the risk of loss of or damage to the goods. Terms begining with "D" refer to arrangements where a seller bears all costs and risks associated with delivering goods to the country of destination. A term begining with "E" refers to any arrangement where the buyer assumes all the costs and risks associated with transporting goods to the country of destination. Terms begining with "F" refer to arrangements where a seller delivers goods to a carrier chosen and paid by a buyer.

CFR Cost and Freight (named port of destination) - A sales arrangement in which a seller quotes a price for goods that includes the cost of transportation to a named port of destination. The CFR term requires the seller to clear the goods for export, but the risk of loss of or damage to the goods due to events occuring after the time the goods have been put on board the vessel is transferred from the seller to the buyer when the goods pass the ship's rail in the port of shipment. The cost of insurance is left to the buyer's account. CFR is used for ocean shipments only.

CIF Cost, Insurance and Freight (named port of destination) - A sales arrangement in which a seller quotes a price for goods that includes insurance, all transportation, and miscellaneous charges to a point of destination for the vessel. The seller arranges for insurance and pays the insurance premium. CIF is used for ocean shipments only.

CIP Carriage and Insurance Paid To (named destination) - Unlike CIF, CIP covers any mode of transport including multimodal transport. The seller has all the obligations which a seller would have under CPT, but must also obtain cargo insurance against the buyer's risk of loss of, or damage to, the goods during the carriage. The seller arranges for insurance and pays the insurance premium.

CPT Carriage paid to (named destination) - A sales arrangement used in place of CFR for shipment by modes other than water. As with a CFR contract, under CPT the seller pays the freight for carriage of goods to a named destination. However, the risk of loss of or damage to goods, as well as any additional costs, is transferred from the seller to the buyer when the goods have been delivered into the custody of the first carrier. CPT arrangements can be used for all modes of transport including multimodal operations and container or "roll on-roll off" traffic by trailer and ferries.

DAF Delivered at Frontier (named place) - Under a DAF arrangement, the seller's obligation ends when goods have been cleared for export at the named place at the frontier (border). It is the buyer's obligation to clear goods for import at the customs border of the importing country. This term is primarily used when goods are transported by rail or road, but it may be used for any mode of transport.

DDP Delivered Duty Paid (named place of destination) A sales arrangement in whch the seller is required to bear all the risks and costs, including duties, taxes and other charges, and clear goods for import. A DDP arrangement imposes maximum obligations on a seller. A DDP contract may be used irrespective of the mode of transport.

DDU Delivered Duty Unpaid (named place of destination) - A sales arrangement in which the seller is responsible for the costs and risks involved in bringing goods to the named place, *excluding* duties, taxes, importation charges, and costs of customs formalities. The buyer is required to pay those costs, and any additional costs, and to bear any risks resulting from a failure to clear the goods for import promptly. A DDU arrangement may be used irrespective of the mode of transport.

DEQ Delivered Ex Quay (Duty Paid) (named port of destination) - A sales arrangement in which the seller bears all risks and costs including duties, taxes, and other delivery charges to the named port of destination, unless otherwise specified. The parties may choose, for example, to exclude some of the costs, such as value added tax (VAT), from the seller's obligations. DEQ arrangements are only used in connection with sea or inland waterway transport.

DES Delivered Ex Ship (named port of destination) - Under a DES contract, the seller bears all costs and risks involved in bringing the goods to a named port of destination and for clearing the goods for export, while the buyer pays import charges. DES arrangements are only used in connection with sea or inland waterway transport.

EXW Ex Works (named place) - A sales arrangement in which the buyer pays all exporting and importing charges, unless otherwise specified. The seller is only responsible for the actual delivery of the goods to the specified destination (i.e. works, factory, warehouse, etc.). This term may be applied to any mode of transport including multimodal.

FAS Free Alongside Ship (named port of shipment) - A sales arrangement in which the seller quotes a price for goods that includes charges for delivery of the goods alongside a vessel at the port of departure. The seller handles the cost of unloading and wharfage. Loading, ocean transportation, and insurance are left to the buyer. FAS requires the buyer to clear the goods for export. FAS is only used for sea or inland waterway transport.

FCA Free Carrier (named place) - A sales arrangement in which a seller is required to deliver goods into the care of a carrier named by the buyer at the designated place, and to clear the goods for export. This term is primarily used for air and rail transport.

FOB Free on Board (named port of shipment) - A sales arrangement in which a seller quotes a buyer a price that covers all costs up to and including delivery of goods aboard a vessel at a designated port of debarkation. The seller is also responsible for export clearance. The buyer is then responsible for all costs and risks involved from that point. The seller is under no obligation to provide insurance or contract of carriage. FOB is only used for sea or inland waterway transport.

APPENDIX VIII

USEFUL WEBSITES

Agency for International Development (AID)
www.info.usaid.gov
Asian-Pacific Economic Cooperation (APEC)
www.apecsec.org.sg
Association of Caribbean States (ACS)
www.acs-aec.org
Association of South East Asian Nations (ASEAN)
www.aseansec.org
Bureau of Export Administration (BXA)
www.bxa.doc.gov
Caribbean Economic Community (CARICOM)
www.caricom.org
Canadian International Trade Tribunal (CITT)
www.citt.gc.ca
China Economy
www.chinaeco.com
China Ministry of Foreign Trade and Economic Cooperation
www.moftec.gov.cn
Commerce Business Daily (CBD)
www.cbd.savvy.com
Consumers for World Trade (CWT)
www.cwt.org
Department of Agriculture
www.usda.gov
Department of Commerce (DOC)
www.doc.gov

Department of Energy (DOE)
www.doe.gov
Department of Treasury
www.ustreas.gov
European Bank for Reconstruction and Development (EBRD)
www.ebrd.com
European Free Trade Association (EFTA)
www.efta.int
European Union (EU)
www.europa.eu.int
Export-Import Bank (EXIM)
www.exim.gov
Federal Trade Commission
www.ftc.gov
Global Information Infrastructure Commission (GIIC)
www.gii.org
Inter-American Development Bank (IADB)
www.iadb.org
International Chamber of Commerce (ICC)
www.iccwbo.org
International Court of Justice (ICJ)
www.icj-cij.org
International Finance Corporation (IFC)
www.ifc.org
International Labor Organization (ILO)
www.ilo.org
International Monetary Fund (IMF)
www.imf.org.
International Telecommunications Union (ITU)
www.itu.ch
International Trade Administration (ITA)
www.ita.doc.gov
International Trade Commission (ITC)
www.usitc.gov
Japanese External Trade Organization (JETRO)
www.jetro.go.jp
Korea Trade Promotion Corporation (KOTRA)
www.kotra.or.kr

Latin American Integration Association (ALADI)
    www.aladi.org [documents in Spanish]
Library of Congress
    www.loc.gov
London International Financial Futures & Options Exchange (LIFFE)
    www.liffe.com
Ministry of International Trade and Industry (Japan) (MITI)
    www.miti.go.jp
Multilateral Investment Guarantee Agency (MIGA)
    www.miga.org
National Trade Data Bank (NTDB)
    www.stat-usa.gov
North American Free Trade Agreement Secretariat (NAFTA)
    www.nafta-sec-alena.org
North American Industrial Classification System (NAICS)
    www.census.gov/epcd/www/naics.html
Office of Defense Trade Controls (ODTC)
    www.pmdtc.org
Organization for Economic Cooperation and Development (OECD)
    www.oecd.org
Organization of Petroleum Exporting Countries (OPEC)
    www.opec.org
Overseas Private Investment Corporation (OPIC)
    www.opic.gov
Patent and Trademark Office (PTO)
    www1.uspto.gov
Revenue Canada
    www.rc.gc.ca
Southern Africa Development Community (SADC)
    www.sadcexpo.org
Trade Development Agency (TDA)
    www.tda.gov
United Nations (UN)
    www.un.org
United States Customs Service
    www.customs.ustreas.gov
United States House of Representatives
    www.house.gov

United States Senate
www.senate.gov
United States Trade Representative (USTR)
www.ustr.gov
United States White House
www.whitehouse.gov
World Bank
www.worldbank.org
World Health Organization (WHO)
www.who.org (or) www.who.ch
World Intellectual Property Organization (WIPO)
www.wipo.org
World Trade Organization (WTO)
www.wto.org

The Editor

Thomas F. O'Herron is the editor of the first and second editions of Terms of Trade: The Language of International Trade Policy, Law and Diplomacy. He is an attorney and a member of the District of Colombia, Maryland and New York bars.

A former Foreign Service Officer with specialization in international trade matters, Mr. O'Herron has held several positions in the Office of International Trade of the Department of State. He has served in diplomatic assignments in Africa and Europe, including a three-year stint as Trade Policy Officer at the United States Mission to the European Union in Brussels.

Mr. O'Herron participated in the Tokyo Round of GATT trade negotiations and has served on American negotiating teams in trade talks with the European Union, Canada, Japan, and other countries. He has lectured overseas on international trade, finance, and development at the invitation of the U.S. Information Agency.

Mr. O'Herron was given a Superior Honor Award by the Department of State for his "major contribution to the maintenance of a free and equitable world trading system."